النصرانية والإسلام حسب الكتاب المقدس والقرآن

Christianity and Islam

according to the Bible and the Qur'ân

Naser Al-Moghamis

DARUSSALAM
Global Leader in Islamic Books
Riyadh • Jeddah • Sharjah • Lahore
London • Houston • New York

First Edition May 2002

© **Dar-us-Salam, 2002**

King Fahd National Library Cataloging-in-Publication Data

Al-Moghmis, Naser
    Christianity and Islam according to the Bible
and the Qur'ân - Riyadh,
    112 p; 21 cm.
    ISBN 9960-861-42-2
    1- Islam and Christianity   1-Title
    214.27 dc   1079/23

Legal Deposit number 1079/23
ISBN 9960-861-42-2

Supervised by:
ABDUL MALIK MUJAHID

Headquarters:

P.O. Box: 22743, Riyadh 11416, KSA
Tel: 00966-1-4033962/4043432
Fax:00966-1- 4021659
E-mail: darussalam@naseej.com.sa
Website: http:// www.dar-us-salam.com
Bookshop: Tel & Fax: 00966-1-4614483
          4644945
Branches & Agents:

K.S. A.

● Jeddah: Tel & Fax: 00966-2-6807752
● Al-Khobar: Tel : 00966-3-8692900
          Fax: 00966-3-8691551
U.A.E.

● Tel: 00971-6-5632623 Fax: 00971-6-5632624

PAKISTAN

● 50 Lower Mall, Lahore
  Tel: 0092-42-724 0024 Fax: 7354072

● Rahman Market, Ghazni Street
  Urdu Bazar, Lahore
  Tel: 0092-42-7120054 Fax: 7320703

U. S. A.

● Houston: P.O. Box: 79194 Tx 77279
  Tel: 001-713-722 0419 Fax: 001-713-722 0431
  E-mail: Sales @ dar-us-salam.com
  Website: http:// www.dar-us-salam.com

● New York: 572 Atlantic Ave, Brooklyn
  New York-11217, Tel: 001-718-625 5925

U.K.
● London: Darussalam International Publications Ltd.
  226 High Street, Walthamstow, London E17 7JH U.K.
  Tel: 0044-208 520 2666 Mobile: 0044-794 730 6706
  Fax: 0044-208 521 7645
● Darussalam International Publications Limited
  Regent Park Mosque, 146 Park Road, London Nw8 7RG
  Tel: 0044-207 724 3363

FRANCE

Editions & Librairie Essalam
135, Bd de Ménilmontant- 75011 PARIS (France)
Tél: 01 43 38 19 56 / 44 83 - Fax 01 43 57 44 31
http: www. Essalam.com E-mail essalam@essalam.com

AUSTRALIA

● Lakemba NSW: ICIS: Ground Floor 165-171, Haldon St.
  Tel: (61-2) 9758 4040 Fax: 9758 4030

MALAYSIA

● E&D BOOKS SDN.BHD.-321 B 3rd Floor, Suria Klcc
  Kuala Lumpur City Center 50088
  Tel: 00603-21663433 Fax: 459 72032

SINGAPORE

● Muslim Converts Association of Singapore
  Singapore- 424484
  Tel: 0065-440 6924, 348 8344 Fax: 440 6724

SRI LANKA

● Darul Kitab 6, Nirmal Road, Colombo-4
  Tel: 0094-1-589 038 Fax: 0094-74 722433

KUWAIT

● Islam Presentation Committee
  Enlightment Book Shop
  P.O. Box : 1613, Safat 13017 KUWAIT
  Tel: 00965-244 7526, Fax: 240 0057

CONTENTS

Preface

A religion should not be judged by the opinions and attitudes of its biased enemies. Neither should it be judged by the behavior of some of its nominal followers because there are bad people among every religious group, and making a judgment based on those people is misleading as they may be violating their religion. A religion should rather be judged by its teachings as well as the effects of these teachings on its **real** followers.

Since the Bible is the basis for the teachings of Christianity, and the Qur'ân is the main source of Islamic Religion and Law, this book compares Islam and Christianity according to a comparative study of the Bible and the Qur'ân. This approach ensures that the comparison is based on facts and not on prejudice or misunderstanding.

It should be emphasized that when this book talks about Islam, it does not give exaggerated or insincere information to persuade the reader, but rather presents the real teachings of Islam. Everything mentioned in this book, about Islam, is **supported by Verses from the Qur'ân** which was revealed about fourteen hundred years ago. Likewise, everything mentioned about Christianity is supported by verses from the Bible.

Naser Al-Moghamis
April 2002 (Safar 1423)
Riyadh, Saudi Arabia
almoghamis@yahoo.com

Introduction

For the benefit of Christian readers, this introduction provides some essential information about Islam in addition to the Islamic attitude towards Christianity and the Bible:

Who is Allâh?

Say (O Muhammad): "He is Allâh, the One and Only; Allâh, to Whom the creatures turn for their needs; He begets not, nor was He begotten; and there is none like Him." (Qur'ân, 112:1-4)

'Allâh' is the name of the God of Muslims, Christians and Jews. He is the God of Prophet Moses 'peace be upon him' (pbuh), Prophet Jesus (pbuh), Prophet Muhammad (pbuh) and all the other Prophets. The name 'Allâh' is not a new name, but rather the true name of God. It is used by Muslims as well as Arabic-speaking Christians.

... and say: "We believe in that which has been revealed to us and revealed to you (Jews and Christians); our God and your God is One, and to Him we have submitted (as Muslims)." (Qur'ân, 29:46)

What is the Qur'ân?

The Qur'ân is the literal Word of Allâh revealed to His Prophet Muhammad (pbuh), through the angel Gabriel, about fourteen hundred years ago. The Qur'ân is the eternal miracle of Islam. Allâh has challenged mankind to produce anything to match it or even match one short chapter of it, yet no human has ever been able to meet the challenge.

And if you are in doubt about what We have revealed to Our slave (Muhammad), then produce a chapter of the like thereof, and call your witnesses (supporters and helpers) besides Allâh if you are truthful. (Qur'ân, 2:23)

Since the Qur'ân is the literal Word of Allâh, it exists only in its original Arabic in which it was revealed, and cannot be translated into another language. However, for the benefit of those who do not speak Arabic, the meanings of the Qur'ân can be translated. Therefore, the quotations in this book are not the Qur'ân but only translations of its meanings.

What Does the Word 'Islam' Mean?

The word 'Islam' means **the conscious and peaceful obedience and submission to the Will of the only true God, 'Allâh'.** All religions were named either after their founders or after nations or tribes e.g. Buddhism, Hinduism, Judaism and Christianity, while the name 'Islam' is not associated with any person, tribe or nation but was given by Allâh in the Qur'ân:

This day, I have perfected your religion for you, completed My favor upon you and have chosen for you Islam as your religion. (Qur'ân, 5:3)

The word 'Muslim' is a description; anyone who submits himself to Allâh's Will and obeys Him is a Muslim.

All the Prophets were Muslims because they obeyed Allâh and submitted themselves to His Will. Furthermore, the true followers and companions of those Prophets were Muslims:

Then when Jesus came to know of their disbelief, he said: "Who will be my helpers in Allâh's cause?" The disciples said: " We are the helpers of Allâh (i.e. we will strive in His cause); we believe in Allâh, and bear witness that we are Muslims (i.e. we submit to Allâh). Our Lord! We believe in what You have sent down and we follow the Messenger (Jesus) so write us down among those who bear witness." (Qur'ân, 3:52,53)

Prophet Muhammad (pbuh) said: "Both in this world and in the Hereafter, I am the nearest of all people to Jesus - the son of Mary. The Prophets are paternal brothers; their mothers are different, but their religion is one (Islamic Monotheism)." (Bukhari)

Early Muslims

Prophet Jesus (pbuh) and all the other Prophets from Adam to Muhammad (peace be upon them) were sent with the same Message, to command human beings to worship Allâh alone, and not to join in worship partners with him. Prophet Jesus (pbuh) never claimed divinity. He taught the Oneness of Allâh and confirmed that he was just a Messenger:

Jesus said, "... I am returning to my Father and your Father, to **my God and your God.**" (John 20:17)

By myself **I can do nothing;** I judge only as I hear, and my judgment is just, for I seek not to please myself but him **who sent me.** (John 5:30)

The disciples followed the teachings of Prophet Jesus (pbuh). They worshiped Allâh alone and kept religion pure for Him. They believed and supported Prophet Jesus (pbuh) to such an extent that Allâh held them up as an excellent example to Muslims in the Qur'ân:

O you who believe! Be you helpers (in the cause) of Allâh as said Jesus - son of Mary, to the disciples: "Who will be my helpers in Allâh's cause?" The disciples said: "We are the helpers of Allâh (i.e. we will strive in His cause)! Then a group of the Children of Israel believed and a group disbelieved. So, We gave power to those who believed against their enemies, and they became the victorious. (Qur'ân, 61:14)

Jesus the merciful Prophet (pbuh) commanded his disciples to be kind and merciful and to forgive others. Let the Qur'ân now describe the followers of Prophet Jesus (pbuh):

Then, We sent after them Our Messengers, and We sent Jesus - son of Mary, and gave him the Injeel (Gospel), and placed **compassion** and **mercy** in the hearts of those who followed him. (Qur'ân, 57:27)

Verily, you will find the strongest among mankind in enmity to the believers (Muslims) the Jews and those who are idolaters, and you will find the **nearest in love** to the believers those who say: "We are **Christians.**" That is because amongst them are priests and monks, and **they are not arrogant.** (Qur'ân, 5:82)

After the Ascension of Prophet Jesus (pbuh) to heaven, most of the Christians remained Unitarian. They used to believe in the Oneness of Allâh following the teachings of Prophet Jesus (pbuh) and all the other Prophets. They did not believe in the doctrines of Trinity, Original Sin, Blood Atonement or Divine Sonship of

Prophet Jesus (pbuh). After centuries of persecution against the Unitarian Christians, the Pauline Church prevailed and the teachings of Paul replaced the teachings of Prophet Jesus (pbuh) and Paul became the real founder of today's Christianity.

Paul, the **self-appointed** thirteenth apostle who **never saw Jesus** (pbuh), wrote more Books of the Bible than any other author, while Prophet Jesus (pbuh) **did not write a single word,** as the **original** Gospel revealed by Allâh to Jesus (pbuh) was lost. However, Paul replaced the Gospel of Jesus (pbuh) with a gospel written by him and invented the doctrines of Original Sin, Blood Atonement and Divine Sonship of Prophet Jesus (pbuh). With the exception of few verses, all the verses in Paul's letters are his own words and not the words of Prophet Jesus (pbuh):

Remember that Jesus Christ of the seed of David was raised from the dead, according to **my (Paul) gospel.** (2 Timothy 2:8) (KJV)

After the loss of the original Gospel of Prophet Jesus (pbuh), many gospels were written. These gospels include some of the genuine teachings of Prophet Jesus (pbuh) mixed with people's own texts and interpretations which were influenced by the beliefs of that period. Therefore, it became difficult and sometimes impossible to know which parts came from Allâh and which from people. As a result, Christians deviated from the teachings of Prophet Jesus (pbuh) and followed the teachings of hundreds of monks and priests which resulted in hundreds of religious groups having different beliefs.

The Effects of the Contradictions in the Bible

The errors and contradictions in the Bible make some Christians reject Christianity and view the Bible as merely a historical book. Those people continue their disbelief to the extent that they deny the existence of God and consequently, they do not believe in all the Prophets including Prophet Jesus (pbuh).

Those people **shock the Muslim** more than anyone else, because no Muslim is a Muslim if he or she does not believe in Jesus Christ (pbuh). The Muslim, in compliance with **the Qur'ân,** believes that Jesus (pbuh) was a great Messenger of Allâh, that he brought the dead to life by Allâh's leave, that he healed those born blind and the lepers by Allâh's leave, that he was born without any male intervention and that he was the Christ.

It is true that the errors and contradictions in the Bible mean that the Word of Allâh has been mixed with people's texts and interpretations. However, **they do not mean** that Prophet Jesus (pbuh) was a liar nor that Allâh does not exist! **They do not mean** that Muhammad (pbuh) was a false prophet nor that Islam is not the true religion!

The Purpose of this Book

The purpose of this book is to achieve the following objectives using the Qur'ân and what survived in the Bible from the teachings of the Prophets (peace be upon them), with the help of our common sense, reason and intellect:

- To confirm that Prophet Jesus (pbuh) was a great Messenger of Allâh, that he was the Christ, that he was given the Gospel, that he was born miraculously without a father and that he gave life to the dead by Allâh's leave and healed him who was born blind and the leper by Allâh's leave.

- To confirm that the **original** Gospel revealed to Prophet Jesus (pbuh) was lost and that the existing gospels include few parts of that original Gospel mixed with people's texts and interpretations, which contain a lot of errors and contradictions.

- To disprove misrepresentations and lies in the Bible against Allâh.

- To disprove false charges in the Bible against the Prophets, Lot, Jacob, Moses, Aaron, David, Solomon, and Job (peace be upon them).

- To disprove false charges in the Bible against Prophet Jesus (pbuh).

- To point out the wrong beliefs which were added (intentionally or unintentionally) into the message of Prophet Jesus (pbuh).

- To disprove the doctrines of Trinity, Original Sin, Blood Atonement and Divine Sonship of Prophet Jesus (pbuh).

- To prove that the Qur'ân is the Word of Allâh and the last revealed Book which has never been changed or adulterated.

- To prove that Prophet Muhammad (pbuh) was the awaited Prophet prophesied in the Bible.

- To present the real Islam **through the Qur'ân** and remove lies and misrepresentations wrapped around Islam by its enemies.

Authenticity of the Bible

The belief in the original holy Books revealed to the Prophets before Prophet Muhammad (pbuh) is one of the six pillars of Faith in Islam:

Say (O Muslims): "We believe in Allâh and that which has been sent down to us and that which has been sent down to **Abraham, Ishmael, Isaac, Jacob,** and to the Tribes, and that which has been given to **Moses** and **Jesus**, and that which has been given to the Prophets from their Lord. We make no distinction between any of them, and to Him we have submitted (in Islam)." (Qur'ân, 2:136)

The Qur'ân mentioned the names of some of these Books: Scriptures of Abraham, the Torah, the Zabur (Psalms), and the Injeel (Gospel). The Scriptures of Abraham were completely lost, while some parts of the original Torah, Psalms and Gospel are still preserved in the Bible mixed with what people's own hands wrote, as confirmed in the Qur'ân:

Then woe to those who **write the Book with their own hands** and then say, "**This is from Allâh,**" to purchase with it a little price! Woe to them for what their hands have written and woe to them for that they earn thereby. (Qur'ân, 2:79)

The original Torah and Gospel are the literal Word of Allâh revealed to his Prophets Moses and Jesus (peace be upon them - pbut), whereas the books of the Bible are merely narratives or stories written in the third person, i.e., the sayings and deeds of the Prophets were written by historians and not by the Prophets themselves. For example, the book of **Deuteronomy** is one of the five books attributed to Prophet Moses (pbuh). If this book was really revealed to Prophet Moses (pbuh) or even written by him, how could it mention **his death**:

And Moses the servant of the Lord **died** there in Moab, as the Lord had said. He **buried him in Moab**, in the valley opposite Beth Peor, but **to this day no-one knows where his grave is. Moses was a hundred and twenty years old when he died** ... (Deuteronomy 34:5-7)

The Gospel revealed to Prophet Jesus (pbuh) was lost and many gospels were written. The church chose four gospels (Matthew,

Mark, Luke and John) and destroyed or banned the rest. Although these gospels include some fragments of the original Gospel, it is very clear that none of them is the Gospel of Prophet Jesus (pbuh), because:

* All the four gospels contain many contradictions and errors[1] while the Gospel of Prophet Jesus (pbuh) which is the Word of Allâh was free from contradictions and errors.

* These gospels are different accounts or reports of the life of Prophet Jesus (pbuh), written by men. They mention his birth, his alleged crucifixion and death, etc, **which cannot be mentioned in the Gospel revealed to Prophet Jesus (pbuh) during his mission**.

Authenticity of the Qur'ân

Allâh has promised to protect the Qur'ân from corruption and adulteration:

No doubt We have sent down the Qur'ân and surely We will guard it (from corruption). (Qur'ân, 15:9)

Allâh has truly fulfilled His Promise and for more than fourteen hundred years, not a single word or even letter has been changed. The Qur'ân exists in its original Arabic text and not even mixed with the words of Prophet Muhammad (pbuh). It is purely and completely the Word of Allâh.

No honest scholar, Muslim or non-Muslim has ever raised any doubt about the purity and genuineness of the Qur'ân. The Qur'ân has been transmitted to us in the most reliable ways. It was written down and learnt by heart by hundreds of people during the lifetime of Prophet Muhammad (pbuh). One of the copies of the Qur'ân which was written few years after the death of Prophet Muhammad (pbuh) is still in existence in Tashkent. Furthermore, since the time of Prophet Muhammad (pbuh), thousands and hundreds of thousands of Muslims have memorized the Qur'ân in succession.

---

(1) See Page 101

God

Does God Relax?

What the Bible Says

... for in six days the Lord made heaven and earth, and on the seventh day he **rested**, and was **refreshed**. (Exodus 31:17) (KJV)

... on the seventh day he (God) **rested** from all his work. (Genesis 2:2)

What the Qur'ân Says

And indeed We created the heavens and the earth and all between them in six days **and nothing of fatigue touched Us**. So bear with patience (O Muhammad) all that they say, and glorify the praises of your Lord, before the rising of the sun and before setting. And during a part of the night glorify His praises and after the prayers ...

We are best aware of what they say. And you (O Muhammad) are not the one to force them (to belief); but warn by the Qur'ân him who fears My threat. (Qur'ân, 50:38-45)

God's Power

What the Bible Says

Jacob Wrestles with God!!!

Then the man said, "Your name will no longer be Jacob, but Israel, because you have **struggled with God** and with men **and have overcome**." (Genesis 32:28)

What the Qur'ân Says

They have not estimated Allâh His Rightful Estimate. Verily, Allâh is All-Strong, All-Mighty. (Qur'ân, 22:74)

Can God be Seen?

What the Bible Says

So Jacob called the place Peniel, saying, " It is because **I saw God face to face**, and yet my life was spared. " (Genesis 32:30)

Moses and Aaron, Nadab and Abihu, and the seventy elders of Israel went up and **saw the God of Israel** ...(Exodus 24:9,10)

Contradicting Verses from the Bible

But, he (God) said, " **You cannot see my face**, for no-one may see me and live. " (Exodus 33:20)

No-one has ever seen God ... (1 John 4:12)

What the Qur'ân Says

No vision can grasp Him, but He grasps all vision. (Qur'ân, 6:103)

God's Description

What the Bible Says

... they trembled because he (God) was angry. **Smoke rose from his (God) nostrils; consuming fire came from his (God) mouth**, burning coals blazed out of it. (2 Samuel 22:8,9)

- **[God rides an angel (cherub)]**

And **he (God) rode upon a cherub, and did fly**: and he was seen upon the wings of the wind. (2 Samuel 22:11) (KJV)

What the Qur'ân Says

And who can be more unjust than he who **invents a lie** against Allâh. (Qur'ân, 6:93)

There is nothing like Him; and He is the All-Hearer, the All-Seer. (Qur'ân 42:11)

So invent not similitudes for Allâh (as there is nothing similar to Him, nor He resembles anything). Truly, Allâh knows and you know not. (Qur'ân, 16:74)

Is God Unjust?

What the Bible Says

... **Awake**, my God; **decree justice**. (Psalm 7:6)

Why does the Almighty not set times for judgment? ... (Job 24:1)

Let God weigh me in honest scales and he will know that I am blameless. (Job 31:6)

then know that **God has wronged me** and drawn his net around me. Though I cry, 'I've been wronged!' I get no response; though I call for help, **there is no justice**. (Job 19:6,7)

What the Qur'ân Says

Truly, Allâh wrongs not mankind in aught, but mankind wrong themselves.(Qur'ân, 10:44)

Surely, Allâh wrongs not even of the weight of an atom, but if there is any good deed, He doubles it and gives from Him a great reward. (Qur'ân, 4:40)

Think not that Allâh is unaware of what the wicked do, but He gives them a respite till a Day when eyes will stare in terror. (Qur'ân, 14:42)

Does God Sleep?

What the Bible Says

Then the Lord **awoke as from sleep**, as a man wakes from the stupor of **wine**. (Psalm 78:65)

Awake, O Lord! Why do you **sleep**? Rouse yourself! ... (Psalm 44:23)

What the Qur'ân Says

Allâh, none has the right to be worshiped but He, the Ever Living, the One who sustains and protects all that exists. Neither slumber nor sleep overtakes Him. To Him belongs whatever is in the heavens and whatever is on the earth. (Qur'ân, 2:255)

Is God Unhelpful?

What the Bible Says

Hear my prayer, O Lord, listen to my cry for help; **be not deaf** to my weeping ... (Psalm 39:12)

Why do you **hide your face** and **forget** our misery and oppression? (Psalm 44:24)

What the Qur'ân Says

And when My slaves ask you (O Muhammad) concerning Me, then I am indeed close (to them). **I respond to the prayer of the supplicant when he calls on Me.** So, let them obey Me and believe in Me, so that they may be led aright. (Qur'ân, 2:186)

Is not He best Who responds to the soul distressed when it calls on Him, and Who removes the evil, and makes you inheritors of the earth? Is there any god with Allâh? Little is that you heed! (Qur'ân, 27:62)

Does God have a Family?

What the Bible Says

... This is what the **Lord** says: **Israel is my firstborn son...** (Exodus 4:22)

The Lord saw this and rejected them because he was angered by his **sons** and **daughters**. (Deuteronomy 32:19)

- **(God married Jerusalem and his wife became a prostitute!)**

This is what the sovereign Lord says to Jerusalem: ... I passed by and saw you kicking about in your blood ... I made you grow like a plant of the field ... Your **breasts were formed** and your hair grew, you who were **naked** and bare. Later I passed by, and when I looked at you and saw that you were **old enough for love**, I spread the corner of my garment over you and covered your nakedness... and you became mine. ...

But you trusted in your beauty and used your fame to become a **prostitute** ... At the head of every street you built your lofty shrines and degraded your beauty, **offering your body with increasing promiscuity to anyone** who passed by ... You engaged in prostitution with the Assyrians too, because you were **insatiable** ... Then you increased your promiscuity... **You adulterous wife! You prefer strangers to your own husband!** (Ezekiel 16:3-32)

What the Qur'ân Says

And to warn those (Jews, Christians, and pagans) who say:

"Allâh has begotten a son." No knowledge have they of such a thing, nor had their fathers. Grievous is the word that comes out of their mouths. They utter nothing but a lie. Perhaps, you would kill yourself (O Muhammad) in grief, over their footsteps (for their turning away from you), because they believe not in this narration (the Qur'ân). (Qur'ân, 18:4-6)

And the Jews and the Christians say: "We are the children of Allâh and His loved ones." Say: "Why then does He punish you for your sins?" Nay, you are but human beings of those He has created, He forgives whom He wills and He punishes whom He wills. And to Allâh belongs the dominion of the heavens and the earth and all that is between them; and to Him is the return. (Qur'ân, 5:18)

And they (Jews, Christians and pagans) say: "Allâh has begotten a son." Glory is to Him. Nay, to Him belongs all that is in the heavens and on earth, and all surrender with obedience (in worship) to Him. The Originator of the heavens and the earth. When He decrees a matter, He only says to it: "Be" and it is. (Qur'ân, 2:116-117)

Say (O Muhammad): He is Allâh, the One and Only; Allâh, to whom the creatures turn for their needs; He begets not, nor was He begotten; and there is none like Him. (Qur'ân, 112:1-4)

The Prophets

The Prophets Lot, Jacob, Moses, Aaron, David, Solomon, and Job (peace be upon them) were noble Messengers of Allâh and are mentioned in both the Qur'ân and the Bible. The belief in these Prophets is one of the six pillars of Faith in Islam. Muslims have great respect for them and believe that their truthfulness and good manners are above suspicion. While the Qur'ân mentions them in a lot of praise, which they deserve, the Bible accuses them of great sins, such as, **cheating, adultery, incest, betrayal, worshiping idols** and **blasphemy**. The Muslim is shocked at these false charges against the Prophets. If normal people do not commit these sins, how far the Prophets are from doing that!

The Prophets were specially prepared and chosen by Allâh to deliver His Message and to be good examples for people to follow. The Prophets embodied in their own speech and actions the teachings they were preaching. Could a Prophet command people to worship Allâh alone, while his heart is turned after other gods? Could he command people to do the right and avoid the wrong, while he commits great sins? Could he command men not to look at women lustfully, while he commits adultery? This is totally unimaginable! Accusing the Prophets of these great sins is an indirect insult to Allâh Who chose and prepared them to convey His Message and guide people to the right way of belief, worship and behavior. The allegation that the Prophets committed great sins means that Allâh wants people to commit these sins because people are commanded to obey the Prophets and follow their example!

These fabricated stories about the Messengers of Allâh spread corruption and evil deeds on earth. If the Messengers of Allâh committed these great sins, then how could the wicked people be punished or even blamed for committing such sins?

Truly, the Muslim's heart overflows with sorrow that the Torah, the Book of Allâh which was revealed as a shining light and guidance, has been changed into a book full of fabricated stories accusing Allâh's Messengers of great sins.

Prophet Moses and Prophet Aaron (pbut)

What the Bible Says

On that same day the Lord told **Moses**, ... This is because **both of you broke faith with me** in the presence of the Israelites at the waters of Meribah Kadesh in the Desert of Zin and because **you did not uphold my holiness** among the Israelites. (Deuteronomy 32:48-51)

So all the people took off their ear-rings and brought them to **Aaron. He took what they handed him and made it into an idol** cast in the shape of a calf, fashioning it with a tool. Then they said, "**These are your gods**, O Israel, who brought you up out of Egypt." (Exodus 32:3,4)

What the Qur'ân Says

And mention in the Book **Moses**. Verily, he was chosen and he was a Messenger, a Prophet. And We called him from the right side of the Mount, and made him draw near to Us for a talk with him. **And We granted him his brother Aaron, a Prophet, out of Our Mercy.** (Qur'ân, 19:51-53)

O you who believe! Be not like those (Jews) who annoyed **Moses**, but Allâh cleared him of that which they alleged, and he was honorable before Allâh. (Qur'ân, 33:69)

And **Aaron** indeed had said to them beforehand: "O my people! You are being tested in this, and verily, **your Lord is (Allâh) the Most Gracious, so follow me and obey my order.**" They said: "We will not stop worshiping it (the calf), until Moses returns to us." (Qur'ân, 20:90,91)

And We gave them the clear Scripture. And guided them to the Right Path. And We left for them (a goodly remembrance) among the later generations. Peace be upon **Moses** and **Aaron**. Verily, thus do We reward the good-doers. Verily, they were two of Our believing slaves. (Qur'ân, 37:117-122)

Prophet Lot (pbuh)

What the Bible Says

That night **they got their father to drink wine**, and the older daughter went in and **lay with him**. He was not aware of it when she lay down or when she got up. ... So **both of Lot's daughters became pregnant by their father**. (Genesis 19:33-36)

What the Qur'ân Says

And Ishmael and Elisha and Jonah and **Lot** and each one of them we **preferred above all creation**. (Qur'ân, 6:86)

And **Lot**, We gave him right judgment and knowledge ... And We admitted him to Our Mercy; truly, **he was of the righteous**. (Qur'ân, 21:74,75)

Prophet Solomon (pbuh)

What the Bible Says

As Solomon grew old, his wives **turned his heart after other gods**, and his heart was not fully devoted to the Lord his God, as the heart of David his father had been. **He followed Ashtoreth the goddess of the Sidonians, and Molech the detestable god of the Ammonites** ...On a hill east of Jerusalem, Solomon built a high place for Chemosh the detestable god of Moab,.... (1 Kings 11:4-7)

What the Qur'ân Says

And to David We gave **Solomon. How excellent a slave!** Verily, he was ever oft-returning in repentance! (Qur'ân, 38:30)

Indeed We gave knowledge to David and **Solomon**, and they both said: "All the praises and thanks are to Allâh, Who has preferred us above many of His believing slaves!" (Qur'ân, 27:15)

Prophet Jacob (pbuh)

What the Bible Says

- **(Jacob lied to get Isaac's blessing)**

... **Jacob said** to his father, "**I am Esau** your firstborn ... Please sit up and eat some of my game so that you may give me your blessing." ... When Isaac caught the smell of his clothes, he blessed him (Jacob).

... Esau said, "... He (Jacob) has **deceived me these two times**: He took my birthright, and now he's taken my blessing!" (Genesis 27:19-36)

The Lord has a charge to bring against Judah; **he will punish Jacob** according to his ways and repay him according to his deeds. **In the womb he grasped his brother's heel**; as a man **he struggled with God**. He struggled with the angel and overcame him; he wept and begged for his favour ... (Hosea 12:2-4)

What the Qur'ân Says

And We bestowed upon him Isaac and **Jacob** each one **We made righteous**. And We made them leaders, guiding by Our Command, and **We revealed to them the doing of good deeds**, performing Salat (prayer), and the giving of Zakat (charity) and they were worshipers of Us (alone). (Qur'ân, 21:72,73)

And remember Our slaves, Abraham, Isaac, and Jacob, owners of strength (in worshiping Us) and of religious understanding. Verily, We did choose them by granting them the remembrance of the Hereafter. And they are with Us, verily, of the chosen and the best. (Qur'ân, 38:45-47)

Prophet David (pbuh)

What the Bible Says

One evening David got up from his bed and walked around on the roof of the palace. From the roof he saw a woman (the wife of Uriah) bathing. The woman was very beautiful... Then David sent messengers to get her. She came to him, and **he slept with her** ... Then she went back home. The woman conceived and sent word to David, saying, "I am pregnant."...

In the morning David wrote a letter to Joab and sent it with Uriah. In it he wrote, "Put Uriah in the front line where the fighting is fiercest. Then withdraw from him so that he will be struck down and die."...

When Uriah's wife heard that her husband was dead, she mourned for him. (2 Samuel 11:2-26)

What the Qur'ân Says

Indeed We gave knowledge to **David** and Solomon, and they both said: "All the praises and thanks are to Allâh, Who has preferred us above many of His believing slaves!" (Qur'ân, 27:15)

Be patient (O Muhammad) of what they say, and remember Our slave David, endowed with power, Verily, **he was ever oft-returning in all matters and in repentance** (toward Allâh). (Qur'ân, 38:17)

We made his (David) kingdom strong and gave him **wisdom and sound judgment in speech and decision**. (Qur'ân, 38:20)

For him (David) is a near approach to Us, and a beautiful place of final return (Paradise). (Qur'ân, 38:25)

Prophet Job (pbuh)

What the Bible Says

After this, Job opened his mouth and cursed the day of his birth. (Job 3:1)

I will say to God: do not condemn me, but tell me what charges you have against me. Does it please you to oppress me... while you smile on the schemes of the wicked? (Job 10:2,3)

...then know that God has wronged me and drawn his net around me. Though I cry, 'I've been wronged!' I get no response; though I call for help, **there is no justice.** (Job 19:6,7)

Why does the Almighty not set times for judgment? (Job 24:1)

Let God weigh me in honest scales and he will know that I am blameless (Job 31:6)

For he (Job) says, 'It profits a man nothing when he tries to please God.' (Job 34:9)

What the Qur'ân Says

And remember Our slave Job, when he invoked his Lord (saying): "Verily, **Satan** has touched me with distress (by ruining my health) and torment (by ruining my wealth)!" (Allâh said to him:) "Strike the ground with your foot: This is (a spring of) water to wash in, cool and a (refreshing) drink." And We gave him (back) his family, and along with them the like thereof, as a mercy from us, and a reminder for those who understand ...

Truly, **We found him patient. How excellent a slave!** Verily, he was ever oft-returning in repentance (to Us)! (Qur'ân, 38:41-44)

Prophet Jesus (pbuh)

While many verses in the Bible exaggerate in praising Prophet Jesus (pbuh) and elevate him into divinity, many other verses accuse him of what is not suitable for him. In contrast, in the entire Qur'ân, there is not a single Verse that attributes any inappropriate behavior to Prophet Jesus (pbuh). The Qur'ân honors Prophet Jesus (pbuh) and mentions him in a lot of praise to the extent that Muslims' eyes stream with tears when they recite the Verses of the Qur'ân which talk about him. Whenever Muslims mention the name of Prophet Jesus, they say 'peace be upon him' (**pbuh**). Muslims love Prophet Jesus (pbuh) to the degree that they name their children after him and his mother Mary.

The Genealogy of Prophet Jesus (pbuh)

What the Bible says

A record of the **genealogy** of Jesus Christ **the son of David** ... (Matthew 1:1)

... He (Jesus) was the **son**, so it was thought, **of Joseph,** the son of Heli (Luke 3:23)

Remember Jesus Christ, raised from the dead, **descended from David** ... (2 Timothy 2:8)

What the Qur'ân Says

She (Mary) said: "O my Lord! How shall I have **a son when**

no man has touched me." He said: "So (it will be,) for Allâh creates what He wills. When He has decreed something, He says to it only: **"BE!" and it is.**" And He will teach him the Book and wisdom, and the Torah and the Gospel. And will make him a Messenger unto the Children of Israel (saying): "I have come to you with a sign from your Lord, that I make for you out of clay the likeness of a bird, and I breathe into it and it becomes a bird by Allâh's leave; and I heal him who was born blind, and the leper, and I bring the dead to life by Allâh's leave. And I inform you of what you eat and what you store in your houses. Surely, therein is a sign for you, if you believe. (Qur'ân, 3:47-49)

Commentary

Although some verses in the Bible say that Prophet Jesus (pbuh) was miraculously conceived from the Holy Spirit, many other verses say that Prophet Jesus (pbuh) is the son of Joseph and that he descended from Prophet David (pbuh) the descendant of Perez who was born of Incest committed by Judah and his daughter-in-law Tamar.

The Qur'ân confirms that Prophet Jesus (pbuh) was born miraculously without any male intervention. Prophet Jesus (pbuh) has no genealogy. He is neither the son of Joseph nor the son of David; he is the son of Mary.

Was Prophet Jesus (pbuh) Crucified and Cursed?

What the Bible says

Christ redeemed us from the curse of the law by becoming **a curse** for us, for it is written: "Cursed is everyone who is hung on a tree." (Galatians 3:13)

What the Qur'ân Says

When the angels said: "O Mary! Allâh gives you the glad tidings of a Word from Him, his name will be the Messiah Jesus, the son of Mary, **held in honor in this world** and in the Hereafter, and of the company of those nearest to Allâh." (Qur'ân, 3:45)

And because of their saying (in boast): "We killed the Messiah Jesus, son of Mary," the Messenger of Allâh, **but they killed him not, nor crucified him but the likeness of him** was put on another man (and they killed that man). And those who differ therein are full of doubts. They have no knowledge, they follow nothing but conjecture. For surely, they killed him not. But Allâh raised him up into Himself. And Allâh is Ever All-Powerful, All-Wise. (Qur'ân, 4:157-158)

Commentary

The Bible says that Prophet Jesus (pbuh) was **crucified** to bear God's wrath for the sins of the believers and accordingly **he was cursed**. On the contrary, Muslims believe, according to the Qur'ân, that he was neither crucified nor cursed but was held and will be held in honor in this life and in the Hereafter.

Prophet Jesus' Behavior Towards His Mother

What the Bible says

And when they wanted wine, the **mother of Jesus** saith unto him, They have no wine. Jesus saith unto her, **Woman, what have I to do with thee?** mine hour is not yet come. (John 2:3,4) (KJV)

Someone told him (Jesus), "Your mother and brothers are standing outside, wanting to speak to you." He replied to him, "**Who is my mother**, and who are my brothers?" Pointing to his disciples, he said, "Here are my mother and my brothers. (Matthew 12:47-49)

What the Qur'ân Says

He (Jesus) said: "Verily, I am a slave of Allâh, He has given me the Scripture and made me a Prophet; and He has made me blessed wheresoever I be, and has enjoined on me prayer, and charity, as long as I live. And **kind to my mother,** and made me not overbearing or miserable." (Qur'ân, 19:30-32)

Commentary

The Qur'ân affirms that Prophet Jesus (pbuh) was kind to his mother. For the Muslim, it is totally unbelievable that Prophet Jesus (pbuh) called his mother '**Woman!**' and that he ignored her when she wanted to speak to him.   If Allâh has commanded us to be kind to our mothers even if they are unbelievers:

And We have enjoined on man to be good to his parents. **His**

mother bore him in weakness upon weakness, and his weaning is in two years; give thanks to Me and to your parents; unto Me is the final destination. But if they strive with you to make you join in worship with Me others that of which you have no knowledge, then obey them not; but behave **with them in this life kindly** (Qur'ân, 31:14-15)

How could we then believe that Prophet Jesus (pbuh) behaved in this way towards his mother Mary who was the best and most righteous woman on earth:

And when the angels said, "O Mary! Verily, Allâh has chosen you, purified you and chosen you **above the women of all nations**." (Qur'ân, 3:42)

Prophet Jesus' Behavior Towards People

What the Bible says:

[Jesus said:]

... A wicked and **adulterous** generation ... (Matthew 12:39)

You **snakes**! You **brood of vipers**! ... (Matthew 23:33)

You **foolish** people! ... (Luke 11:40)

Jesus turned and said to **Peter**, "Get behind me, **Satan**! ..." (Matthew 16:23)

The (Canaanite) woman came and knelt before him. "Lord, help me!" She said. He (Jesus) replied, "**It is not right to take the children's bread and toss it to their dogs**." (Matthew 15:25,26)

But those enemies of mine who did not want me to be a king over them—bring them here and **kill them in front of me**. (Luke 19:27)

What the Qur'ân Says

And when Jesus came with clear Proofs, he said: "I have come to you **with wisdom**, and to make plain some of that concerning which you differ. So fear Allâh and obey me." (Qur'ân, 43:63)

"And kind to my mother, and made me not **overbearing** or miserable." (Qur'ân, 19:32)

Commentary

According to the Bible, Prophet Jesus (pbuh) used to insult his people and even his disciples. Furthermore, Prophet Jesus (pbuh) is reported as saying that the Canaanites are the dogs of Israel.

In contrast, the Qur'ân indicates that Prophet Jesus (pbuh) was kind and wise in his behavior towards his people.

The Mission of Prophet Jesus (pbuh)

What the Bible says

[Jesus said:]

... I did not come to bring peace, but a sword. For I have come to turn a man against his father, a daughter against her mother, ... (Matthew 10:34,35)

I have come to bring fire on the earth, and how I wish it were already kindled! (Luke 12:49)

If anyone comes to me and does not **hate his father and mother, his wife and children, his brothers and sisters**–yes, even his own life–he cannot be my disciple. (Luke 14:26)

What the Qur'ân Says

And in their footsteps we sent Jesus the son of Mary, confirming the law that had come before him and We bestowed on him the Gospel, therein was **guidance** and **light**. (Qur'ân, 5:46)

Then, We sent after them Our Messengers, and We sent Jesus son of Mary, and gave him the Injeel (Gospel), and **placed compassion and mercy in the hearts of those who followed him**. (Qur'ân, 57: 27)

Commentary

According to the Qur'ân, Prophet Jesus (pbuh) was sent as guidance and light for Israel. He came to bring peace and not to kindle fire. Prophet Jesus (pbuh) did not encourage his disciples to hate their fathers and mothers but commanded them to be kind to them. The disciples followed the teachings of Prophet Jesus (pbuh) to the extent that Allâh has honored them with everlasting praise in the Qur'ân for their compassion and mercy.

The Divinity of Prophet Jesus (pbuh)

What the Bible Says

In the beginning was the Word, and the Word was with God, and the **Word was God**. (John 1:1)

He is the image of the invisible God, the firstborn over all creation. For by him all things were created ... For **God was pleased to have all his fullness dwell in him**. (Colossians 1:15-19)

... when God brings his firstborn into the world, he says, "**Let all God's angels worship him**." (Hebrews 1:6)

... Jesus Christ our **only sovereign and Lord**. (Jude: 4)

What the Qur'ân Says

And to warn those (Jews, Christians, and pagans) who say, "**Allâh has begotten a son**." No knowledge have they of such a thing, nor had their fathers. **Grievous** is the word that comes out of their mouths. They utter nothing but a lie. Perhaps, you would kill yourself (O Muhammad) in grief, over their footsteps (for their turning away from you), because they believe not in this narration (the Qur'ân). (Qur'ân, 18:4-6)

And when Allâh will say (on the Day of Judgment): "O Jesus, son of Mary! Did you say unto people: Worship me and my mother as two gods besides Allâh?" He will say "Glory to You! **It was not for me to say what I had no right (to say)**. Had I said such a thing, You would surely have known it. You know what is in my inner-self though I do not know what is in Yours; truly You, only You, are the All-Knower of all that is hidden. Never did I say to them aught except what You did command me to say: **'Worship Allâh, my Lord and your Lord.'** And I was a witness over them while I dwelt amongst them, but when you took me up, You were the watcher over them; and You are a witness to all things." (Qur'ân, 5:116-117)

Verily, the likeness of Jesus before Allâh is the likeness of Adam. He created him from dust, then said to him: "Be," and he was. (Qur'ân, 3:59)

Surely, they have disbelieved who say: "Allâh is the Messiah Jesus, son of Mary." But the Messiah Jesus said: "O Children of Israel! Worship Allâh, my Lord and your Lord." Verily, whosoever sets up partners (in worship) with Allâh, then Allâh has forbidden Paradise to him, and the Fire will be his abode. And for the polytheists and wrongdoers there are no helpers.

Surely, disbelievers are those who say: "Allâh is the third of the three (in a Trinity)." But there is no god but one God. And if they cease not from what they say, verily, a painful torment will befall on the disbelievers among them. Will they not turn with repentance to Allâh and ask His Forgiveness? For Allâh is Oft-Forgiving, Most Merciful.

The Messiah, son of Mary, was no more than a Messenger; many were the Messengers that passed away before him. His mother was a woman of truth. **They both used to eat food** (as any other human being, while Allâh does not eat). Look how We make the revelations clear for them; yet look how they are deluded away (form the truth). Say (O Muhammad): "How do you worship besides Allâh something which has no power either to harm or benefit you? But it is Allâh who is the All-Hearer, All-Knower."

Say (O Muhammad): "O people of the Scripture! Exceed not the limits in your religion other than the truth, and do not follow the vain desires of people who went astray before and who misled many, and strayed from the Right Path." (Qur'ân, 5:72-77)

Do they attribute as partners to Allâh those who created nothing but they themselves are created? (Qur'ân, 7:191)

Commentary

Why is Prophet Jesus (pbuh) called God?

- **Is it because he was born without a father?** Then **Adam** was created without a father or mother, **Eve** was created without a mother and according to the Bible, "**Melchizedek**" is without father or mother, without genealogy, without beginning of days or end of life! (Hebrews 7:1-3)

- **Is it because he gave life to the dead?** Then Elisha did more than that. According to the Bible, Elisha gave life to the dead (2 Kings 4:32-35) and when a man's body was thrown into Elisha's tomb, the body touched Elisha's bones and the man came to life and stood up on his feet. (2 Kings 13:21)

- **Is it because Jesus (pbuh) is called in the Bible "the son of God"? Then, according to the Bible**, God has many sons and daughters, and a **wife** also (Glorified is He, and High Exalted above that!):

... This is what the Lord says: **Israel is my firstborn son** (Exodus 4:22)

The Lord saw this and rejected them because he was angered by his **sons** and **daughters**. (Deuteronomy 32:19)

... he (Jesus) began to teach them, saying: ... Blessed are the peacemakers, for they will be called **sons of God**. (Matthew 5:2,9)

You adulterous wife! You prefer strangers to your own **husband (God)!** (Ezekiel 16:2-32)

What then made people believe in the divinity of Prophet Jesus (pbuh)?

The Jewish literature is full of metaphors. They speak and write in a metaphorical language to make the description more powerful. Prophet Jesus (pbuh), Prophet Jacob (pbuh) and many other righteous people were called the **sons of God** to emphasize their strong belief in God. They even called Jerusalem "**the wife of God**" to emphasize God's love for it. The following verses in the Bible clarify the meaning of "**son of God**":

Yet to all who **received him**, to those who **believed in his name**, he gave the right to become **children of God**— children born not of natural descent, nor of human decision or a husband's will, but born of God. (John 1:12,13)

The concept of the **Divine** Sonship of Prophet Jesus (pbuh) may well have resulted from the misunderstanding of the Jewish way of speaking and writing coupled with the effect of pagan concepts at that time about sexual relations between gods and women.

Prophet Jesus (pbuh) never claimed divinity or equality with Allâh. On the contrary, he emphasized his humanity and confirmed that he was just a Messenger of Allâh:

- **Prophet Jesus (pbuh) confirmed the Oneness of Allâh**

  "The most important one," answered Jesus, "is this: 'Hear, O Israel, **the Lord our God, the Lord is one**." (Mark 12:29)

- **Prophet Jesus (pbuh) confirmed that he was a Messenger of Allâh**

  Jesus answered, "My teaching is not my own. It comes from him who sent me." (John 7:16)

  But Jesus said to them, "Only in his home town and in his own house is **a prophet** without honour." (Matthew 13:57)

- **Prophet Jesus (pbuh) used to pray to his God and our God**

  ... he (Jesus) said to them, "Sit here while I go over there and pray." ... Going a little farther, he **fell with his face to the ground and prayed** ... (Matthew 26:36,39)

  During the days of Jesus' life on earth, **he offered up**

prayers and petitions with loud cries and tears **to the one who could save him from death** and he was heard because of his reverent submission. (Hebrews 5:7)

- **Prophet Jesus (pbuh) was a servant of Allâh**

  Here is my **servant** (Jesus) whom I have chosen ... (Matthew 12:18)

- **Prophet Jesus (pbuh) confirmed his humanity and denied divinity**

  By myself **I can do nothing** ... (John 5:30)

  No-one knows about that day or hour, not even the angels in heaven, **nor the Son**, but only the Father. (Matthew 24:36)

  Jesus said, "... I am returning to my Father and your Father, to **my God and your God.**" (John 20:17)

  [Peter said:]

  Men of Israel, listen to this: Jesus of Nazareth was a man accredited by God to you ... (Acts 2:22)

- **Prophet Jesus (pbuh) attributed his miracles to Allâh**

  ... I drive out demons **by the finger of God** ... (Luke 11:20)

  ... Jesus looked up and said, "Father, I thank you that you have **heard me.**" (John 11:41)

- **Prophet Jesus (pbuh) refused to be called 'good', let alone being called 'God'!**

  A certain ruler asked him, "Good teacher, what must I do to inherit eternal life?" "Why do you call me good?" Jesus answered. **"No-one is good–except God alone."** (Luke 18:18,19)

The Day of Judgment

According to the Old Testament

What the Bible Says

For the living know that they will die, but the dead know nothing; **they have no further reward** ... Go, eat your food with gladness, and drink your wine with a joyful heart ... **What ever your hand finds to do, do it with all your might** ... (Ecclesiastes 9:5-10)

...then know that God has wronged me and drawn his net around me. Though I cry, 'I've been wronged!' I get no response; though I call for help, **there is no justice**. (Job 19:6,7)

Why does the Almighty not set times for judgment? ... (Job 24:1)

What the Qur'ân Says

Did you then think that We had created you in jest, and that you would not be brought back to us (for account)? (Qur'ân, 23:115)

Not without purpose did We create heaven and earth and all between! That is the thought of the unbelievers! But woe to the unbelievers from the Fire.

Shall We treat those who believe and work deeds of righteousness, the same as those who spread corruption on earth? Shall We treat the pious as the wicked? (Qur'ân, 38:27,28)

Commentary

Although, every Prophet commanded his people to believe in life after death, there is almost no mention of the Day of Judgment, in the Old Testament. Furthermore, many verses in the Old Testament deny life after death and consequently encourage people to enjoy the life of this world lawfully or unlawfully. This wrong belief confirms that the Torah and the teachings of the Prophets, have been changed by the materialistic Jews.

The denial of life after death did shake the Jews' belief in Allâh and His justice. Therefore, they accused Allâh of injustice and lack of mercy. Because many Jews had no belief in punishment and reward after death, all kinds of evil and crime spread among them to the extent that they killed many Prophets and tried to kill Prophet Jesus (pbuh).

In the Qur'ân, Allâh confirms that He created us for a purpose and that this life is a test and preparation for the eternal life after death. On the Day of Judgment, Allâh will fulfill His justice and bring all humans to account. He will punish the wicked people and will shower His mercy on the righteous people who obeyed Him and did good deeds.

In this life many wicked people disobey Allâh and commit sins and crimes against innocent people, yet they live a happy life. In contrast, many righteous people are persecuted and killed unjustly. Is Allâh unaware of that? No, Allâh only delays the punishment and reward until the Day of Judgment. On the Day of Judgment, Allâh will reward the righteous people who believed in Him, followed His commands and suffered for His sake. He will punish the evildoers who disobeyed Him, killed innocent people, spread corruption and led people astray. On that day, the people who were wronged will get revenge.

According to the New Testament

What the Bible Says

For the Son of Man is going to come in his Father's glory with his angels, and then he will reward each person according to what he has done. I tell you the truth, **some who are standing here will not taste death before they see the Son of Man coming in his kingdom."** (Matthew 16:27,28)

… They will see the Son of Man coming on the clouds of the sky, with power and great glory. And he will send his angels with a loud trumpet call, and they will gather his elect from the four winds, from one end of the heavens to the other … I tell you the truth, **this generation will certainly not pass away until all these things have happened.** (Matthew 24:30-34)

… **some who are standing here will not taste death** before they see **the kingdom of God** come with power. (Mark 9:1)

What the Qur'ân Says

They ask you about the Hour (Day of Resurrection): "When will be its appointed time?" Say: " The knowledge thereof is with my Lord. None can reveal its time but He." (Qur'ân, 7:187)

Commentary

The New Testament says that Jesus (pbuh) told his disciples that **their generation would not pass away** until the kingdom of God comes and each person is rewarded according to what he had done. Their generation and tens of generations passed away and these things have not happened!

Did Prophet Jesus (pbuh) lie or did the writers of the books?

Muslims believe in Prophet Jesus (pbuh) and believe that everything he said was true because it was revelation from Allâh who sent him.

Allâh states in the Qur'ân that no one knows the time of the Day of Judgment except Him. Prophet Jesus (pbuh) declared that he had no knowledge of its appointed time:

No-one knows about that day or hour, not even the angels in heaven, **nor the Son**, but only the Father. (Matthew 24:36)

Women

Women's Nature

What the Bible Says

A man ought not to cover his head, since **he is the image and glory of God; but the woman is the glory of man**. (1 Corinthians 11:7)

What the Qur'ân Says

Never will I allow to be lost the work of any of you, male or female. You are one of another. (Qur'ân, 3:195)

Commentary

The Qur'ân confirms that men and women are equal in the sight of Allâh. The Qur'ân does not say that the man is the glory of Allâh and the woman is the Glory of man. This is nonsense because the male and the female are both created by Allâh, and because the male comes from the female and the female comes from the male. **They are one of another.**

Women's Original Sin

What the Bible Says

And Adam was not the one deceived; **it was the woman who was deceived and became a sinner.** (1 Timothy 2:14)

What the Qur'ân Says

And he (Satan) swore by Allâh to them both (Adam and Eve) (saying): "Verily, I am one of the sincere well-wishers for you both." So he misled them with deception. (Qur'ân, 7:21-22)

Thus **did Adam disobey his Lord**, so he went astray. Then his Lord chose him, and turned to him with forgiveness, and gave him guidance. (Qur'ân, 20:121,122)

Commentary

According to the Qur'ân both Adam and Eve were tempted by Satan. The Qur'ân blames both of them for their sin. However, Adam and Eve prayed earnestly to Allâh for forgiveness and He forgave them.

According to the Bible, Eve was the sinner and because of her sin all humans are born in sin.

Women's Veil

What the Bible Says

If a woman does not cover her head, she should have her hair cut off; and if it is a disgrace for a woman to have her hair cut or shaved off, she should cover her head. A man ought not to cover his head, since **he is the image and glory of God; but the woman is the glory of man.** For man did not come from woman, but woman from man; neither was man created for woman, but woman for man. **For this reason,** and because of the angels, the woman **ought to have a sign of authority on her head.** (1 Corinthians 11:6-10)

What the Qur'ân Says

O Prophet! Tell your wives and your daughters and the women of the believers to draw their cloaks (veils) all over their bodies. That will be better, that **they should be known so as not to be annoyed.** (Qur'ân, 33:59)

And when you ask them (the wives of the Prophet) for anything you want, ask them from behind a curtain: **that is purer for your hearts and for their hearts.** (Qur'ân, 33:53)

Commentary

The Bible instructs women to cover their heads. The purpose of the covering is to show the authority of men over them because men are the image and glory of Allâh while women are the glory of men! Because of this teaching, some non-Muslims think that Muslim women, who wear the veil, are ill-treated and neglected.

Unlike the Bible, the Qur'ân instructs women to wear the veil for their protection. The veil is one of the Islamic measures to create a righteous society and to block the roads leading to fornication and adultery. The Qur'ân clarifies that the veil makes wicked men stay away from women. Furthermore, the veil purifies the heart from immoral thoughts and temptation because showing beauty may excite men's sexual feelings. On the other hand, the Qur'ân allows women to show their beauty to other women, their husbands and some close relatives in addition to children and male servants who have no sexual desire.

Women's Role

What the Bible Says

Now I want you to realise that the head of every man is Christ, **and the head of the woman is man,** and the head of Christ is God. (1 Corinthians 11:3)

I do not permit a woman to teach or to have authority over a man; she must be silent. For Adam was formed first, then Eve. And Adam was not the one deceived; **it was the woman who was deceived and became a sinner.** (1 Timothy 2:12-14)

If a **man sells his daughter** as a servant, she is not to go free as menservants do. (Exodus 21:7)

No widow may be put on the list of widows unless she is over sixty ... and is well known for her good deeds, such as bringing up children, showing hospitality, **washing the feet of the saints** ... (1 Timothy 5:9,10)

What the Qur'ân Says

And they (women) have rights (over their husbands) similar to the rights against them, in kindness, but men have a degree (of responsibility) over them. And Allâh is All-Mighty, All-Wise. (Qur'ân, 2:228)

Men are the protectors and maintainers of women, because Allâh has made one of them to excel the other, and because they spend of their property (for the support of women). (Qur'ân, 4:34)

And give the women on marriage their dowry (money given by the husband to his wife) with a good heart. (Qur'ân, 4:4)

Commentary

The Bible and the Qur'ân are in agreement on the headship of the man over the family. However, they differ in the reasons for the man's headship and the powers of this headship.

The Bible makes the husband the head of the wife because the man is the glory of Allâh while the woman is the glory of man, and because the woman was deceived and became a sinner. According to the Bible, a woman is not allowed to teach or have authority over a man and must be silent; good women are those who **wash the feet of saints**; and what is more, **a man can sell his daughter** and she is not to go free!

Islam treats the man and the woman equally. The woman has rights similar to those of the man. However, Islam assigns to the man and the woman responsibilities which suit their physiological and psychological qualities. The man as a head of the family has a duty to earn money to provide his wife and children with all the requirements of life such as accommodation, food and clothes. The woman is assigned the task of keeping house and bringing up future generations. **The woman in Islam is not responsible for any financial obligation.** She is not burdened with any duties other than her house and children.

Since no organization can work successfully without a leader, the husband is appointed as leader of the family which is a small organization. Without a leader, the family will be in complete disorder and marriage may end in divorce. Islam appoints the husband as head of the family for two reasons stated in the above Verse: firstly, the man's natural qualities are more suitable for this responsibility and secondly, the man bears all the financial requirements to support his family.

Women's Testimony

What the Bible Says

If a man takes a wife and, after lying with her, dislikes her and slanders her and gives her a bad name, saying, "I married this woman, but when I approached her, **I did not find proof of her virginity**," then the **girl's father and mother shall bring proof** that she was a virgin to the town elders at the gate... Then her parents shall **display the cloth** before the elders of the town ... If, however, the charge is true and no proof of the girl's virginity can be found, she shall be brought to the door of her father's house and there the men of her town **shall stone her to death** ... (Deuteronomy 22:13-21)

What the Qur'ân Says

And for those who accuse their wives, but have no witnesses except themselves, let the testimony of one of them be four testimonies (i.e. testifies four times) swearing by Allâh that he is one of those who speak the truth. And the fifth (testimony should be) the invoking of the Curse of Allâh on him if he is of those who tell a lie. **But it shall avert (turn away) the punishment from her, if she bears witness four times by Allâh, that he is telling a lie.** And the fifth should be that the Wrath of Allâh be upon her if he speaks the truth. (Qur'ân, 24:6-9)

And those who accuse chaste women, and produce not four witnesses, **flog them (the accusers) with eighty stripes and reject their testimony forever.** (Qur'ân, 24:4)

Verily, those who accuse chaste, believing women, who never

even think of anything touching their chastity, are cursed in this life and in the Hereafter, and for them will be great torment. (Qur'ân, 24:23)

Commentary

According to the judgment of the Bible, if a man accuses his wife of not being a virgin, the wife's father and mother have to bring proof that she was a virgin, otherwise, the wife will be stoned to death! **The wife's testimony carries no weight!**

According to the judgment of the Qur'ân, if a man accuses his wife of committing adultery, the wife can nullify the accusation as her testimony is accepted, consequently, the wife will not be punished. However, if the accuser is not her husband, then he has to bring four witnesses. If not, he will receive eighty lashes and his testimony will be rejected forever.

Women's Righteousness

What the Bible Says

... I found one upright man among a thousand, but **not one upright woman among them all.** (Ecclesiastes 7:28)

Then the cover of lead was raised, and there in the basket sat **a woman!** He said, **"This is wickedness,"**... (Zechariah 5:7,8)

The woman Folly is loud; she is undisciplined and without knowledge. (Proverbs 9:13)

What the Qur'ân Says

And Allâh has set forth an example to those who believe: The wife of Pharaoh, when she said: "My Lord! Build for me a home with You in Paradise, and save me from Pharaoh and his work, and save me from the people who do wrong." And **Mary**, the daughter of Imran who guarded her chastity. And We breathed into (the sleeve of her garment) through Our Ruh (Gabriel), and she testified to the truth of the Words of her Lord, and His Scriptures, and she was one of the devout servants. (Qur'ân, 66:11,12)

Commentary

The Bible states that women are foolish, wicked, undisciplined and without knowledge. It also says that no one upright woman was found among them all. On the contrary, the Qur'ân orders all Muslims, men and women, to follow the shining examples of two perfect women, Mary the mother of Jesus (pbuh) and Pharaoh's wife. These two ideal women were models of faith, righteousness, and patience for the sake of Allâh.

Women's Inheritance

What the Bible Says

(The daughters of Zelophehad said to Moses), "Our father died .. and left no sons. Why should our father's name disappear from his clan because he had no son? Give us property among our father's relatives." So Moses brought their case before the Lord and the Lord said to him .. "**If a man dies and leaves no son, give his inheritance over to his daughter.** If he has no daughter, give his inheritance to his brothers. If he has no brothers, give his inheritance to his father's brothers. If his father had no brothers, give his inheritance to the nearest relative in his clan, that he may possess it."... (Numbers 27:1-11)

What the Qur'ân Says

There is a share for men and a share for women from what is left by parents and those nearest related, whether, the property be small or large a legal share. (Qur'ân, 4:7)

Allâh commands you concerning your children's (inheritance): to the male, a portion equal to that of two females. (Qur'ân, 4:11)

For parents (father and mother), **a sixth share of inheritance to each** if the deceased left children. (Qur'ân, 4:11)

Commentary

According to the laws of inheritance in the Bible, the woman has no right to inherit, whether she is a mother, a sister, a wife or a daughter except for the daughter who has no brothers. This law was in use until the last century and some high-class families in Europe still give most of their possessions to the first-born son. The woman in Islam has a share of inheritance. The daughter's portion is half that of the son. This share is very generous given that, in Islam, the man's financial obligations are by far more than those of the woman. The man gives the dowry to his wife. He pays for all the necessities of life such as accommodation, food and clothes. He supports his parents in addition to his wife and children. On the other hand, the wife does not have to support anyone even herself because her husband is responsible for maintaining her, **no matter how rich she is.** It is worth noting that in some cases the woman's share of inheritance is equal to that of the man.

What the Bible Says

When a woman has her regular flow of blood, the impurity of her monthly period will last seven days, **and anyone who touches her will be unclean till evening.** Anything she lies on during her period will be unclean, and anything she sets on will be unclean. ... Whoever touches anything she sits on must wash his clothes and bathe with water, and he will be unclean till evening. (Leviticus 15:19-22)

When a woman has a discharge of blood for many days at a time other than her monthly period .... She will be unclean as long as she had the discharge, ... On the eighth day she must take two doves or two young pigeons and bring them to the priest ... The priest is to sacrifice **one for a sin offering** and the other for a burnt offering. In this way he will make **atonement** for her before the Lord for the uncleanness of her discharge. (Leviticus 15:25-30)

What the Qur'ân Says

They ask you (O Muhammad) concerning menstruation. Say: it is Adha (harmful to the husband if he has sexual intercourse with his wife during her period), so keep away from women during menstruation and go not in unto them till they are cleansed. And when they have purified themselves, then go in unto them as Allâh has enjoined upon you. Truly Allâh loves those who turn unto Him, and loves those who keep themselves pure and clean. (Qur'ân, 2:222)

Commentary

The Bible describes woman's period as if it is a highly contagious disease which can be passed to other people by touch. In addition, woman's discharge of blood is considered a sin of which a woman has to repent!

In Islam, woman's period or discharge of blood is neither considered a sin nor transmittable uncleanness. The husband and the wife can do everything except sexual intercourse, as it is harmful according to the Qur'ân.

Other Teachings and Beliefs

The Source of Religion

What the Bible Says

When the apostles in Jerusalem heard that Samaria had accepted the word of God, they sent Peter and John to them. When they arrived, they prayed for them that they might receive the Holy Spirit, because the Holy Spirit had not yet come upon any of them; they had simply been baptized into the name of the Lord Jesus. Then **Peter and John placed their hands on them, and they received the Holy Spirit**. (Acts 8:14-17)

While Peter was still speaking these words, **the Holy Spirit came on all who heard the message.** The circumcised believers who had come with Peter were astonished that the gift of the **Holy Spirit had been poured out even on the Gentiles.** For they heard them speaking in tongues and praising God. Then Peter said, "… **They have received the Holy Spirit just as we have.**" (Acts 10:44-47)

When the day of Pentecost came, they were all together in one place .. **All of them were filled with the Holy Spirit** and began to speak in other tongues as the Spirit enabled them ...

Then Peter stood up with the Eleven, raised his voice and addressed the crowd: ... **this is** what was spoken by the prophet Joel:

In the last days, God says, I will pour out my Spirit on all people. Your sons and daughters will prophesy, your young men will see visions, your old men will dream dreams. (Acts 2:1-17)

... Philip the evangelist, one of the Seven. He had four unmarried **daughters who prophesied**. (Acts 21: 8,9)

What the Qur'ân Says

And who can be more unjust than he who invents a lie against Allâh, or says: "a revelation has come to me" whereas no revelation has come to him in anything; and who says, "I will reveal the like of what Allâh has revealed." And if you could but see when the wrongdoers are in the agonies of death, while the angels are stretching forth their hands (saying): "Deliver your souls! This day you shall be recompensed with the torment of degradation because of what you used to utter against Allâh other than the truth. And you used to reject His Ayat (proofs, evidences, verses, signs, revelations, etc.) with disrespect. (Qur'ân, 6:93)

They (Jews and Christians) took their rabbis and their monks to be their Lords besides Allâh (by obeying them in things which they made lawful or unlawful according to their own desires without being ordered by Allâh), and (they also took as their Lord) the Messiah, son of Mary, while they were commanded to worship none but One God, there is no god but He. Praise and glory is to Him from having the partners they associate (with Him)." (Qur'ân, 9:31)

Commentary

People cannot know Allâh's Will and cannot know the right way of belief and worship by their own means. Therefore, Allâh has sent His Messengers to all nations. Those Messengers were specially chosen and prepared by Allâh Himself to convey His Divine Message and guide people to the Right Way. The Muslim believes in all the Prophets and makes no distinction between one another because the religion taught by all the Prophets was pure Islam (the submission to the Will of Allâh).

When people deviate from the teachings of the Prophets and depend on themselves and their limited knowledge, they stray from the Right Path and sink into paganism and idol worship. Some people take the sun as their god, some worship idols and some worship a man as their god besides Allâh, and all these people believe that they are right!

According to the Bible, Allâh's revelation was not restricted to the Prophets only. The Holy Spirit guided and inspired the Church and its members because the promised gift of the Holy Spirit was poured out on the followers of Christ at Pentecost (Acts 2:1).

Furthermore, the gift of the Holy Spirit was not limited to the apostles of Prophet Jesus Christ (pbuh), but was given to all the believers, men and women, young and old, Israelites and non-Israelites; and consequently people were able to prophesy and speak in tongues as the Holy Spirit was speaking through them. (Matthew 10:19,20; Acts 8:14-17; Acts 10:44-47; Acts 11:1; Acts 2:1-41)

What are the results of this loose concept of inspiration?

- Tens of gospels were written and preached. Each one of them contradicts the other (Galatians 1:6; 2 Corinthians 11:4)

- Many people appointed themselves as **apostles of Christ**. Each one of them preached a different gospel and cursed other apostles and accused them of being false apostles, deceitful workmen, masquerading as apostles of Christ (2 Corinthians 11:13)

- Christianity has been divided into hundreds of sects and denominations and every one of them claims to be implementing the Will of Allâh through the Holy Spirit.

- Many Christians overlooked the teachings of Prophet Jesus

(pbuh) and followed the teachings of Paul who **never saw Jesus** (pbuh) and never consulted the disciples of Prophet Jesus (pbuh), (Galatians 1:11-16). Paul wrote more Books of the Bible than any other author, while Prophet Jesus (pbuh) did not write a single word. Paul's letters have no reference to the teachings of Prophet Jesus (pbuh). In fact, Paul's teachings contradict the teachings of Prophet Jesus (pbuh).

- The teachings of Prophet Jesus (pbuh) have been replaced with what people saw in **dreams**. The Law of Allâh which was revealed to Prophet Moses (pbuh) and approved by Prophet Jesus (pbuh) was replaced with dreams. The Law of Allâh forbids the pig and other abominable things, (Leviticus 11:7,8; Isaiah 66:17). However, a dream of Peter cancelled this law and consequently all animals, reptiles and birds were allowed, (Acts 11:5-9). Furthermore, Paul described the "Law of Allâh" as **"the law of sin and death"** (Romans 8:2), and said: "Now that faith has come, we are no longer under the supervision of the **law**." (Galatians 3:25)

- Prophet Jesus (pbuh) taught the Oneness of Allâh and confirmed that he was just a Messenger, and the disciples followed his teachings. However, by the end of the first century and **as a result of the alleged inspiration of the Holy Spirit,** most Christians exalted Prophet Jesus (pbuh) into the divine sphere, and afterwards in the fourth century the doctrine of Trinity was invented and Prophet Jesus (pbuh) became their god besides Allâh.

The Muslim rejects this dogma for many reasons:

- Muslims believe in Prophet Jesus (pbuh) and in the original Gospel revealed to him. They also believe that the true followers of Prophet Jesus (pbuh) were righteous people and are praised in the Qur'ân in many Verses (5:82; 57:27; 61:14; 3:82). However, those followers were not Prophets and did not have the authority to change the religion of Prophet Jesus (pbuh) or replace his Gospel with what their own hands wrote.

- The books of the New Testament have many contradictions. If the Holy Spirit was inspiring the writers of these books, then the books should be consistent!

- If what people see in dreams represents the actual Will of Allâh, then all people are Prophets because all people dream! If people could prophesy, make laws and change the Law of Allâh according to their dreams and according to the alleged inspiration of the Holy Spirit, then why did Allâh send His Prophet Jesus (pbuh) and reveal His Gospel to him?

- The New Testament Books contain many mistakes such as the confirmation that the generation of disciples would not pass away until the kingdom of God comes (Matthew 16:27; Matthew 24:30-35; Mark 9:1). This incorrect prophecy proves that the Holy Spirit did not inspire the writers.

- In Islam, dreams and personal insight are not considered sources of legislation. The concept of revelation in Islam is different; the revelation which represents the Will of Allâh is what Allâh revealed in the Qur'ân and what He revealed to His Messenger Muhammad (pbuh). Islamic Law is based on the Qur'ân and on the sayings and actions of Prophet Muhammad (pbuh) who was guided by inspiration from Allâh. No one can change the Law of Allâh and the teachings of His Prophet Muhammad (pbuh). Muslim scholars have no right either to change the Law of Allâh or to make laws which Allâh has not ordained. Their function is to inform people of what Allâh and His Prophet said, explain the Law of Allâh and guide people to the right path of Allâh following in the footsteps of Prophet Muhammad (pbuh).

Faith and Deeds

What the Bible Says

That if you confess with your mouth, "Jesus is Lord," and believe in your heart that God raised him from the dead, you will be **saved**. (Romans 10:9)

… a man is not justified by observing the law, but **by faith in Jesus Christ** … for if righteousness could be gained through the law, Christ died for nothing! (Galatians 2: 16-21)

Contradicting Verses from the Bible

What good is it, my brothers, if a man claims to have faith but has no deeds? Can such faith save him? (James 2:14)

Faith by itself, if it is not accompanied by action, is **dead**. (James 2:17)

…a person is justified by what he does and not by faith alone. (James 2:24)

What the Qur'ân Says

It will not be in accordance with your desires (Muslims), nor the desires of the people of the Scripture (Jews and Christians), whosoever does wrong, will have the recompense thereof, and will not find against Allâh any protecting friend or helper. And whoever does righteous good deeds, male or female, and is a believer, such will enter Paradise and not the least injustice will be done to them (Qur'ân, 4:123,124)

As for those who disbelieved, their deeds are like a mirage in a desert. The thirsty one thinks it to be water, until he comes up to it, he finds it to be nothing; but he finds Allâh with him, Who will pay him his due (Hell). And Allâh is Swift in taking account. (Qur'ân, 24:39)

Commentary

Paul says "if you confess with your mouth, "Jesus is Lord," and believe in your heart that God raised him from the dead, you will be saved." He also says that **man is justified by faith.**

On the contrary, James says, "Faith by itself, if it is not accompanied by action, is dead" and "a person is justified by what he does and **not by faith alone"**.

The best comment on this contradiction is what Allâh says in the Qur'ân:

Do they not consider the Qur'ân with care? Had it been from other than Allâh, they would surely have found therein much contradiction. (Qur'ân, 4:82)

When Prophet Jesus (pbuh) was asked about the way to have eternal life, he did not say anything about the belief in crucifixion or resurrection. He said, "Obey the Commandments" (Matthew 19:17). He urged on his disciples the importance of deeds, "unless your **righteousness** surpasses that of the Pharisees and the teachers of the law, you will certainly not enter the kingdom of heaven. " (Matthew 5:20). Therefore, Faith, if it is not accompanied by good deeds, is dead.

Both Muslims and true Christians, who followed in the footsteps of Prophet Jesus (pbuh), believe that a person is justified by **faith and deeds**.

The Original Sin

What the Bible Says

For just as through the **disobedience of the one man the many were made sinners**, so also through the obedience of the one man the many will be made righteous (Romans 5:19)

… Christ died for our sins … (1 Corinthians 15:3)

… God was pleased through the foolishness of what was preached to save those who believe. Jews demand miraculous signs and Greeks look for wisdom, but we preach Christ crucified: a stumbling-block to Jews and **foolishness** to Gentiles, but to those whom God has called, both Jews and Greeks, Christ the power of God and the wisdom of God. **For the foolishness of God is wiser than man's wisdom**, and the weakness of God is stronger than man's strength. (1 Corinthians 1:21-25)

… If any one of you thinks he is wise by the standards of this age, he should become a "**fool**" so that he may become wise. (1 Corinthians 3:18)

Contradicting Verses from the Bible

The soul who sins is the one who will die. **The son will not share the guilt of the father, nor will the father share the guilt of the son.** The righteousness of the righteous man will be credited to him, and the wickedness of the wicked will be charged against him.

But if a wicked man turns away from all the sins he has committed and keeps all my decrees and does what is just and right, he will surely live; he will not die. **None of the**

offences he has committed will be remembered against him. Because of the righteous things he has done, he will live. **Do I take any pleasure in the death of the wicked?** Declares the Sovereign Lord ... (Ezekiel 18:20-23)

What the Qur'ân Says

Thus did Adam disobey his Lord, so he went astray. Then his Lord chose him and turned to him with forgiveness and gave him guidance. (Qur'ân, 20:121,122)

Or is he not informed of what is in the Pages (Scripture) of Moses. And of Abraham who fulfilled (all that Allâh ordered him to do or convey): that no burdened person (with sins) shall bear the burden (sins) of another. And that man can have nothing but what he does (good or bad). (Qur'ân, 53:36-39)

Commentary

The Qur'ân says, "And He it is Who accepts repentance from His slaves, and forgives sins, and He knows what you do". The Bible says, " But if a wicked man turns away from all the sins he has committed and keeps all my decrees and does what is just and right, he will surely live; he will not die. **None of the offences he has committed will be remembered** against him .. **Do I take any pleasure in the death of the wicked**"?

The Qur'ân confirms that both Adam and Eve repented of their sin and Allâh forgave them. Even if Allâh did not forgive them, does that mean the inheritance of sin and that all humans are born in sin!

The dogma of the Original Sin was only one of the inventions of Paul and it is against the Bible, the Qur'ân and the teachings of the Prophets. It is against Allâh's Law and all human laws. Prophet Jesus (pbuh) never taught this dogma!

- The Bible says, " The son will not share the guilt of the father".

- The Qur'ân says, " No burdened person (with sins) shall bear the burden (sins) of another. And that man can have nothing but what he does (good or bad)".

- Human laws do not punish the son for the crime of the father.

- Every one of us believes that the son should not be held responsible for what the father does.

Why do we then reject all that and follow Paul. Paul himself admitted that this dogma was foolishness; so, why do we become fools and accept it?

Crucifixion

What the Bible Says

... Christ died for our sins ... (1 Corinthians 15:3)

For just as through the disobedience of the one man the many were made sinners, so also through the obedience of the one man the many will be made righteous. (Romans 5:19)

Contradicting Verses from the Bible

The son will not share the guilt of the father, nor will the father share the guilt of the son. The righteousness of the righteous man will be credited to him, and the wickedness of the wicked will be charged against him. But if a wicked man turns away from all the sins he has committed and keeps all my decrees and does what is just and right, he will surely live; he will not die. **None of the offences he has committed will be remembered** against him. Because of the righteous things he has done, he will live. **Do I take any pleasure in the death of the wicked?** declares the Sovereign Lord. (Ezekiel 18: 20-23)

What the Qur'ân Says

And because of their saying (in boast), "We killed the Messiah Jesus, son of Mary," the Messenger of Allâh, but they killed him not, nor crucified him but the likeness of him was put on another man (and they killed that man). And those who differ therein are full of doubts. They have no knowledge, they follow nothing but conjecture. For surely, they killed him not. But Allâh raised him up into Himself. And Allâh is Ever All-Powerful, All-Wise. And there is not one of the People of the Scripture but will believe in him (Jesus (pbuh), as only a Messenger of Allâh and a human being) before his death, and on the Day of Resurrection he will be a witness against them. (Qur'ân, 4:157-159)

Commentary

The Qur'ân confirms that Prophet Jesus (pbuh) was not crucified but Allâh saved his life and raised him up to heaven. Careful study of the Bible also proves that Jesus (pbuh) was not crucified; and even if Jesus (pbuh) was crucified, does that save humans?

Does the killing of an innocent man and a great Messenger of Allâh save evildoers? Does Allâh say that? Did Jesus (pbuh) say that? Did any Prophet say that? Is that logical?

When Prophet Jesus (pbuh) was asked about the way to have eternal life, he said, "**Obey the Commandments**" (Matthew 19:17). He did not say anything about the belief in crucifixion or resurrection.

Islam rejects this dogma for the following reasons:

- This dogma is an accusation of lack of mercy against Allâh. Allâh is not bloodthirsty and He does not demand bloodshed to forgive the sins of the people who repent. The Qur'ân says, "And verily, I am indeed forgiving to him who repents, believes and does righteous good deeds, and then remains constant in doing them." (Qur'ân, 20:82)

- If Allâh, according to the Bible, does not take any pleasure in the death of the wicked and forgives them if they repent, then how does Allâh take pleasure in the killing of the great Prophet Jesus (pbuh) who was the best and the most righteous one on earth at that time, for a sin committed by someone else? This is the height of injustice and harshness.

Islam declares that no person bears the sins of another; no one is saved by the suffering and crucifixion of another one. Salvation is a personal responsibility. It can be achieved by the belief in the One and Only true God, Allâh, and by following His Commands.

- This dogma necessitates that all the people before the time of Jesus (pbuh) including the Prophets and their followers could not be saved because they did not believe that Prophet Jesus (pbuh) died for their sins!

- Allâh says in the Qur'ân: "And those who differ therein are full of doubts. They have no knowledge, they follow nothing but conjecture". The truthfulness of this Verse is realized by comparing the narratives of the alleged crucifixion in the four gospels, which differ starkly. For the sake of brevity, only three contradictions are listed:

According to Matthew 27:32, **Jesus** carried his own cross.

According to John 19:17, **Simon** carried the cross.

According to Matthew 27:44, the **two** criminals **insulted** Jesus. According to Luke 23:39, one of the criminals insulted Jesus but **the other defended him**

According to Matthew 28:2, after the resurrection:
<u>Two</u> women saw <u>one angel sitting on the stone</u>

According to Luke 24:3,
<u>Many</u> women saw <u>two men standing beside them</u>

According to John 20:12,
<u>one</u> woman saw <u>two angels sitting where Jesus' body had been</u>

According to Mark 16:5,
<u>Three</u> women saw <u>one man sitting on the right side of the tomb</u>

The reason for these contradictions is that the disciples did not witness the alleged crucifixion as, according to the Bible, they all had forsaken Prophet Jesus (pbuh) and run away. (Mark 14:50)

- After the alleged crucifixion, Jesus (pbuh) met the disciples and proved to them that he was alive and had not been crucified. He did eat food to prove that he was not a spirit:

But they were terrified and affrighted, and supposed that they had seen a **spirit**. And he (Jesus) said unto them, Why are ye troubled? and why do thoughts arise in your hearts? Behold my hands and my feet, that it is I myself: handle me, and see; **for a spirit hath not flesh and bones, as ye see me have** ... And they gave him a piece of a broiled fish, and of a honeycomb. And he took it, and **did eat** before them. (Luke 24:37-43) (KJV)

These verses are clear evidence that Prophet Jesus (pbuh) was not crucified and resurrected because Prophet Jesus (pbuh) proved that he was not a spirit, and according to the Bible, the resurrected body is spiritual:

So also is **the resurrection of the dead**. It is sown in corruption; it is raised in incorruption: ... It is sown a natural body, **it is raised a spiritual body**. There is a natural body, and there is a spiritual body (1 Corinthians 15:42-44) (KJV)

Forgiveness

What the Bible Says

When anyone is guilty in any of these ways, he must confess in what way he has sinned ... and **the priest shall make atonement for him for his sin.** (Leviticus 5:5,6)

... Receive the Holy Spirit. If you (the disciples) **forgive anyone his sins, they are forgiven** ... (John 20:22,23)

If a person **sins** and does what is forbidden in any of the Lord's commands, **even though he does not know it,** he is guilty and will be held responsible. He is to bring to the priest as a guilt offering a ram from the flock, one without defect and of the proper value. In this way **the priest will make atonement for him** for the wrong he has committed **unintentionally,** and he will be forgiven. (Leviticus 5:17,18)

... The sin offering is to be slaughtered before the Lord ... **The Priest** who offers it **shall eat it** ... (Leviticus 6:25,26)

What the Qur'ân Says

And He it is Who accepts repentance from His slaves, and forgives sins, and He knows what you do. (Qur'ân, 42:25)

And whoever does evil or wrongs himself but afterwards seeks Allâh's forgiveness, he will find Allâh Oft-Forgiving, Most Merciful. (Qur'ân, 4:110)

And there is no sin for you in the mistakes that you make unintentionally, but what your hearts deliberately intend. And Allâh is Ever Oft-Forgiving, Most Merciful. (Qur'ân, 33:5)

Commentary

The Bible states that if a person commits a sin **unintentionally**, he is guilty and will be held responsible. In Islam, sins committed unintentionally are forgiven.

In Islam, there is no confession except to Allâh alone. The Muslim can ask Allâh for forgiveness without the mediation of saints or priests. Muslim scholars do not have the authority to accept acts of worship or forgive sins on behalf of Allâh. Prophet Muhammad (pbuh) himself did not claim this authority. When Prophet Muhammad (pbuh) asked Allâh to forgive some hypocrites, Allâh said to him in the Qur'ân:

Ask forgiveness for them (O Muhammad), or ask not forgiveness for them; if you ask forgiveness for them seventy times, Allâh will not forgive them. That is because they disbelieved in Allâh and His Messenger, and Allâh guides not those who are perversely rebellious. (Qur'ân, 9:80)

Prophet Muhammad (pbuh) said to his daughter Fatimah:

" O Fatimah, daughter of Muhammad! Rescue yourself from Hell, I can benefit you nothing before Allâh".

Marriage

What the Bible Says

And I say unto you, Whosoever shall put away his wife, except it be for fornication, and shall marry another, committeth adultery: and whoso marrieth her which is put away doth commit adultery.

His disciples say unto him, If the case of the man be so with his wife, it is not good to marry. But he (Jesus) said unto them, All men cannot receive this saying, save they to whom it is given. For there are some eunuchs, which were so born from their mother's womb: and there are some eunuchs, which were made eunuchs of men: **and there be eunuchs, which have made themselves eunuchs for the kingdom of heaven's sake.** He that is able to receive it, **let him receive it.** (Matthew 19:9-12)(KJV)

If anyone comes to me and does not hate his father and mother, his **wife** and children, his brothers and sisters—yes, even his own life—he cannot be my disciple. (Luke 14:26)

Those who marry will face many troubles in this life, and I want to spare you this. (1 Corinthians 7:28)

What the Qur'ân Says

But monasticism[1] they invented. We ordained it not, but (they sought it) only to please Allâh therewith and they did not observe it with the right observance. So We gave those among them who believed, their reward; but many of them are rebellious transgressors. (Qur'ân, 57:27)

(1) The way of life of monks in monasteries; living a very simple life without marriage.

And among His Signs is this, that He created for you wives from among yourselves, that you may find rest in them, and He has put between you love and mercy. Verily, in that are indeed signs for people who reflect. (Qur'ân, 30:21)

Commentary

The Bible recommends celibacy[1] and says that marriage brings many troubles in this life. It also says that Prophet Jesus (pbuh) encouraged his disciples to make themselves eunuchs[2] for the kingdom of heaven's sake.

This act of monasticism could not be taught by Prophet Jesus (pbuh) for the following reasons:·

- Jesus (pbuh) was a Messenger of Allâh and he only taught what Allâh commanded him to teach. The Qur'ân states that monasticism was an invention and Allâh did not ordain it.

- The result of this teaching is the extinction of humans or at least the extinction of the religious people who follow it.

- Celibacy is against human instincts. It suppresses sexual desires, which causes psychological problems and makes life miserable. This teaching made many Christians hate religion and prefer secular life.

In Islam, salvation is not achieved by the suffering of the body and the suppression of emotions. Islam forbids self-persecution and allows enjoying the pleasures of life while observing Allâh's laws. These laws ensure that we get what is beneficial and avoid what is harmful. Islam encourages the Muslim to get married as soon as possible. Prophet Muhammad (pbuh) said, " Whoever is able to marry, should marry." However, Islam prevents humans from descending to the level of animals. Therefore, it forbids adultery and perverted sexual practices which spread diseases, destroy the family, and harm the individual and the entire society.

---

(1) Celibacy is the state of being unmarried and without having sex.
(2) A eunuch is a man who has had part of his sex organs removed.

Polygamy (Polygyny)

What the Bible Says

In Jerusalem David took **more wives**... (1 Chronicles 14:3)

He (Solomon) had **seven hundred** wives (1 Kings 11:3)

What the Qur'ân Says

If you fear that you shall not be able to deal justly with the orphans, then marry women of your choice, two, or three, or four; but if you fear that you shall not be able to deal justly with them, then only one, or slaves that your right hands possess. That is nearer to prevent you from doing injustice. And give the women on marriage their dowry (money given by the husband to his wife) with a good heart. (Qur'ân, 4:3,4)

Commentary

The Bible does not prohibit polygamy and most of the Old Testament Prophets were polygamous. Criticizing polygamy implies criticizing those Messengers, and this should not be acceptable to any true Jew, Christian or Muslim.

Unlike the Bible, the Qur'ân limits polygamy to a maximum of four wives provided that the husband deals with them justly. If not, then only one wife is allowed. Therefore, polygamy is not one of the pillars of Islam but a restricted permission! The Qur'ân did not invent polygamy but limited it.

Islam allows polygamy not merely for the satisfaction of desires but as a solution to certain social problems. It is very clear that if the number of women in any society is equal to the number of men, then every man will marry one woman and as a result, no man can marry more than one woman. However, if the number of women is more than that of men, then polygamy is without doubt better than leaving some women without husbands which may result in fornication, prostitution, homosexuality, diseases, and illegitimate children. Therefore, many women, who could not get married, find in polygamy the right way to satisfy their emotions and enjoy the pleasure of having a family and children.

Incest

What the Bible Says

- **[Prophet Abraham (pbuh) married his sister]**

    Abraham replied .. Besides, she really is **my sister**, the daughter of my father though not of my mother; and **she became my wife.** (Genesis 20:11,12)

- **[Prophet Lot (pbuh) and his daughters]**

    ..That night **they got their father to drink wine**, and the older daughter went in and **lay with him.** He was not aware of it when she lay down or when she got up. .. So **both of Lot's daughters became pregnant by their father.** (Genesis 19:30-36)

- **[Reuben and his father's concubine]**

    While Israel (Jacob) was living in that region, Reuben went in and **slept with his father's concubine** Bilhah, and **Israel heard of it.** (Genesis 35:22)

- **[Judah and his daughter-in-law Tamar]**

    When Judah saw her (Tamar), he thought she was a prostitute, for she had covered her face. Not realizing that she was **his daughter-in-law**, he went over to her by the roadside and said, "**Come now, let me sleep with you.**" ... So he gave them to her and **slept with her and she became pregnant by him.** (Genesis 38:15-18)

Commentary

Incest is a great sin and a betrayal of trust by someone supposed to be a protector not an offender. It is religiously, morally and naturally rejected and detested.

Allâh revealed His Books as light and guidance to lead all humans out of darkness and to warn them and guard them against evil.

These Books command righteous deeds and forbid shameful deeds and wickedness.

It is true that Allâh does mention in His Books crimes and sins committed by some people. However, Allâh mentions these stories to warn people against committing such sins and crimes, and not to encourage people to commit them. When a book mentions very indecent stories of incest or adultery without criticizing or punishing the people who committed them, then the book, in fact, encourages people to do the same. In the Bible:

- ·Prophet Lot (pbuh) is accused of committing incest with his daughters night after night and there is no criticism.

- Judah committed incest with his daughter-in-law Tamar and Allâh rewarded Judah for this crime with two sons born of incest and one of them was (according to the Bible) a great grandfather of Prophet Jesus (pbuh), although he was born miraculously without a father!

- Reuben committed incest with his father's concubine Bilhah, without any reaction from his father Prophet Jacob (pbuh).

What is the moral teaching of these immoral stories? Does any upright person want his or her sons and daughters to read them? These fabricated stories have no benefit except spreading immorality and evil on earth and damaging the reputation of Prophets and righteous people. These stories cannot be the Word of Allâh and cannot be from the teachings of the Prophets.

What the Qur'ân Says

Verily, those who like that illegal sexual intercourse should be spread among the believers, will have a painful torment in this world and in the Hereafter and Allâh knows and you know not (Qur'ân, 24:19)

The Biblical and the Qur'ânic Styles

The Biblical Style

- **Two adulterous sisters**

The word of the Lord came to me: Son of man, there were two women... They became prostitutes in Egypt, engaging in prostitution from their youth. In that land **their breast were fondled and their virgin bosoms caressed.** The older was named Oholah, and her sister was Oholibah ... **Oholah** is **Samaria**, and **Oholibah** is **Jerusalem** ...

When she carried on her prostitution openly and **exposed her nakedness** ... there she lusted after her lovers, <u>**whose genitals**[1] **were like those of donkeys and whose emission was like that of horses**</u>. (Ezekiel 23:1-20)

The Qur'ânic Style

And Allâh puts forward the example of a city enjoying security and quiet, abundantly supplied with sustenance from every place, but it disbelieved in the Favors of Allâh. So Allâh made it taste extremes of hunger and fear, because of that which they used to do. (Qur'ân, 16:112)

As for Aad, they were arrogant in the land without right, and they said: "Who is mightier than us in power?" Did they not see that Allâh Who created them was mightier than them in power? And they used to deny Our Signs. So, We sent against them a furious wind through days of disaster, that We might make them taste the torment of disgrace in the life of this world. And verily, the torment of the Hereafter will be more

_____
(1) The genitals are the sexual organs.

disgracing, and they will not be helped.

And as for Thamud, We gave them guidance, but they preferred blindness to guidance; so the stunning punishment of humiliation overtook them because of what they used to earn. And We saved those who believed and used to fear Allâh, keep their duty to Him and avoid evil. (Qur'ân, 41:15-18)

Commentary

In order to show the seriousness of idolatry and sins committed by Israel and Judah, the Bible pictured Samaria and Jerusalem as two sisters who engaged in prostitution. This prostitution metaphor is often used in the Bible, (Ezekiel 16:2-32; Jeremiah 3:1).

The writer of these verses used very lewd sexual expressions and words which obviously cannot be from Allâh. If any moral person cannot utter these words, then how could we believe that Allâh spoke them!

In contrast, when the Qur'ân talks about the sins committed by some people and their punishment, it uses very noble and impressive language which moves the reader to tears and fills the heart with awe. It does not take long for the reader to recognize the beauty and majesty of the Word of Allâh.

Wisdom and Knowledge

What the Bible Says

For with much wisdom comes much sorrow; the more knowledge the more grief. (Ecclesiastes 1:18)

...The fate of the fool will overtake me also. What then do I gain by being wise?... (Ecclesiastes 2:15)

What the Qur'ân Says

He grants wisdom to whom He wills, and he, to whom wisdom is granted, is indeed granted abundant good. (Qur'ân, 2:269)

Allâh will exalt those who believe among you, and those who **have been granted knowledge,** to high ranks. (Qur'ân, 58:11)

Racism

What the Bible Says

Noah, a man of the soil, proceeded to plant a vineyard. When **he drank some of its wine, he became drunk and lay uncovered inside his tent**. Ham the father of Canaan, saw his father's nakedness and told his two brothers outside ...

When Noah awoke from his wine and found out what his youngest son had done to him, he said, "**Cursed be Canaan**! The lowest of slaves will he be to his brothers." (Genesis 9:20-25)

The (Canaanite) woman came and knelt before him. "Lord, help me!" she said. He (Jesus) replied, "**It is not right to take the children's bread and toss it to their dogs.**" (Matthew 15:25,26)

You may charge a **foreigner** interest, but not a brother **Israelite**... (Deuteronomy 23:20)

What the Qur'ân Says

O mankind! We have created you from a male and a female, and made you into nations and tribes, **that you may know one another.** Verily, the most honorable of you with Allâh is that who is **the most pious of you.** Verily, Allâh is All-Knowing, All-Aware. (Qur'ân, 49:13)

And He has united their (believers') hearts. If you had spent all that is in the earth, you could not have united their hearts, but Allâh has united them. Certainly He is All-Mighty, All-Wise. (Qur'ân, 8:63)

Commentary

According to the Bible, Prophet Noah (pbuh) cursed Canaan and made him a slave for his brothers because of the mistake of his father Ham, which implies that the descendants of Ham (black people) are cursed people and are slaves for the descendants of Shem and Japheth. The Muslim rejects this story for the following reasons:

• Prophet Noah (pbuh) was a great Messenger of Allâh and accusing him of drinking wine and lying naked is not accepted by Muslims.

• Canaan shouldn't have been cursed for Ham's mistake. Why was an innocent son cursed for his father's mistake? This is an accusation of injustice against one of the great Prophets.

• The Jews claim that they are the children of God and the rest of people are gentiles. They fabricated this story to arrogate to themselves superiority over the Canaanites and to give themselves the right to kill and humiliate them.

In addition, the Jew's hands wrote in the Bible that they could charge a foreigner interest, but not a brother Israelite. Further, the Jews falsely accuse Prophet Jesus (pbuh) of saying that the Canaanites are their dogs. It is unbelievable that Jesus (pbuh) said this racist statement. How could a Messenger of Allâh consider non-Israelites as the dogs of the children of Israel?

Every nation throughout history has claimed a kind of superiority based on false criteria such as race, color or language. However, the Qur'ân provides the true criterion which is **piety**. The superiority of a person over another depends on righteousness and good behavior, and not blood, wealth or nationality because all humans are the children of Adam.

The Qur'ân says that Allâh created different races so **that people recognize each other.** He did not do that to give certain races superiority or advantage. In fact, the difference in the shapes and colors of people is one of the miracles of Allâh which deserves admiration and appreciation; although Allâh created us from one male (Adam) and one female (Eve), each person is different from the other; each one is unique. Therefore, the difference is a great miracle of Allâh and not justification for racism.

Prophet Muhammad (pbuh) said:

"O people! Your God is one and your forefather (Adam) is one. An Arab is not better than a non-Arab and a non-Arab is not better than an Arab, and a red (i.e. white) person is not better than a black person and a black person is not better than a red person **except in piety.**"

Prophet Muhammad (pbuh) was the first one to practice this teaching. He treated his Companions equally, the rich, the poor, Arabs and non-Arabs. Bilal the Ethiopian, Suhaib the Roman and Salman the Persian were among the Prophet's closest Companions. Prophet Muhammad (pbuh) said,

"Salman (the Persian) is one of my family."

Killing the Enemy's Women and Children

What the Bible Says

This is what the **Lord almighty says**: "... Now go, attack the Amalekites and totally destroy everything that belongs to them. Do not spare them; **put to death men and women, children and infants, cattle and sheep, camels and donkeys.**" (1 Samuel 15:2,3)

Now **kill all the boys.** And **kill every woman** who has slept with a man, but save for yourselves every girl who has never slept with a man. (Numbers 31:17,18)

However, in the cities of the nations the Lord your God is giving you as an inheritance, **do not leave alive anything that breathes.** (Deuteronomy 20:16)

What the Qur'ân Says

Allâh does not forbid you to deal justly and kindly with those who fought not against you on account of religion nor drove you out of your homes. Verily, Allâh loves those who are just. Allâh forbids you only those who fought against you on account of religion, and have driven you out of your homes, and helped to drive you out, that you make friends of them. And whosoever makes friends of them, then such are the wrongdoers. (Qur'ân, 60:8,9)

Commentary

The Bible asserts that Allâh and His Prophets Moses and Joshua, peace be upon them, commanded the Jews to kill guiltless women and children!

And they say: "This is from Allâh," but it is not from Allâh: and they speak a lie against Allâh while they know it. (Qur'ân, 3:78)

There is no doubt that Allâh is free from these shocking crimes and so are His Prophets. Allâh and His Prophets never commanded the killing of blameless women and children. Allâh says in the Qur'ân:

For that cause, We ordained for the Children of Israel that if anyone killed a human being for other than murder or spreading mischief in the land, **it would be as if he killed all mankind**, and if anyone saved a life, it would be as if he saved the life of all mankind. And indeed, there came to them Our Messengers with clear signs, even then after that many of them continued to exceed the limits in the land. (Qur'ân, 5:32)

In the Qur'ân, there is not a single Verse that commands the killing of the enemy's women or children. On the contrary, the Qur'ân instructs Muslims to deal justly and kindly with all innocent people. Prophet Muhammad (pbuh) used to warn his army, saying, "Do not kill an old man, a woman or a child."

Languages

What the Bible Says

Now the whole world had one language and a common speech. As men moved eastward, they found a plain in Shinar and settled there. .... Then they said, "Come, let us build ourselves a city, with a tower that reaches to the heavens..."

But **the Lord came down to see the city and the tower** that the men were building. The Lord said, "If as one people speaking the same language they have begun to do this, then nothing they plan to do will be impossible for them. Come, **let us go down and confuse their language so they will not understand each other.**" (Genesis 11:1-7)

What the Qur'ân Says

And among His signs is the creation of the heavens and the earth, and the **difference of your languages** and colors. Verily, in that are indeed signs for men of sound knowledge. (Qur'ân, 30:22)

Commentary

According to the Bible, the difference in languages was a plot from God who felt jealous and afraid when He saw men speaking the same language.

Allâh says in the Qur'ân that the difference of languages and colors is one of His miracles because He created humans and gave them the ability to speak, listen and understand. Therefore, the difference in languages is a miracle, and not a curse. Allâh does not plot jealously against humans. All humans cannot do anything against the Will of Allâh and can neither harm nor benefit the Almighty Allâh whether they speak one language or not.

Worship

What the Bible Says

Praise the Lord with the harp; make music to him on the **ten-stringed lyre**. Sing to him a new song; **play skillfully, and shout for joy**. (Psalm 33:2,3)

Praise the Lord... Praise him with the sounding of the trumpet, **praise him with the harp and lyre**, praise him with the tambourine and **dancing**, praise him with the strings and flute, praise him with the clash of cymbals... (Psalm 150:1-5)

What the Qur'ân Says

And of mankind is he who purchases idle talks (i.e. music, singing) to mislead from the path of Allâh without knowledge, and takes it by way of mockery. For such there will be a humiliating torment. (Qur'ân, 31:6)

Not all of them are alike; a party of the People of the Scripture (Jews and Christians) stand for the right, they recite the Verses of Allâh during the hours of the night, prostrating themselves in prayer. (Qur'ân, 3:113)

O you who have believed! Bow down, and prostrate yourselves, and worship your Lord and do good that you may be successful. (Qur'ân, 22:77)

Only those believe in Our revelations, who, when they are reminded of them, fall down prostrate, and glorify the praises of their Lord, and they are not arrogant. Their sides forsake their beds, to invoke their Lord in fear and hope, and they spend (in charity) out of what We have bestowed on them. No person knows what delights of the eye are kept hidden for them as a reward for what they used to do. Is then he who is a believer like him who is rebellious and wicked? They are not alike. (Qur'ân, 32:15-18)

Those were they unto whom Allâh bestowed His Grace from among the Prophets, of the offspring of Adam, and of those whom We carried with Noah, and of the offspring of Abraham and Israel, and from among those whom We guided and chose. When the Verses of the Most Gracious (Allâh) were recited unto them, they fell down prostrate and weeping. Then there has succeeded them a later generation who have ruined worship and have followed lusts. So they will be thrown in Hell. Except those who repent and believe, and work righteousness. Such will enter Paradise and will not be wronged in the least. Eden Paradise, which the Most Gracious (Allâh) has promised to His slaves in the Unseen. Verily, His Promise must come to pass. (Qur'ân, 19:58-61)

Commentary

The purpose of worship in Islam is to purify and cleanse the soul and daily life of sin and evil. The most fundamental and the most important act of worship is 'Salah', which is the five daily prayers. These daily prayers strengthen attachment to Allâh and remind of commitments to Him. They help to prevent the Muslim from being dragged into unlawful worldly activities. The prayers are performed five times a day to ensure this purification.

Recite what has been revealed to you of the Book (Qur'ân), and perform worship (prayers). Verily, worship prevents from great and shameful sins and evil wicked deeds. (Qur'ân 29:45)

Performing prayer in congregation in mosques creates among the Muslims bonds of love and equality. The poor and the rich, the low and the high the black and the white, all stand shoulder to shoulder and prostrate themselves before their Lord; racial pride and arrogance die out. They stand in full devotion and humility reciting the Verses of the Qur'ân, giving thanks to Allâh and asking Him for forgiveness and help without intermediaries and without priests. No other faith can be like Islam in this close, direct and noble relationship with Allâh. In the mosque there is no priests claiming the authority to forgive sins on behalf of Allâh and turning the hearts of people from pure worship of the one God. In the mosque there is no music to occupy the mind and divert it away from clear thinking and understanding.

Furthermore, worship, in Islam, is not limited to the mosque only. Every good action is considered an act of worship if it is performed sincerely for the sake of Allâh and according to His Law. Even dealings with parents, relatives and people can be acts of worship if they are done according to the instructions of Allâh and for His Pleasure. Prophet Muhammad (pbuh) said:

"Removing obstructions and dirt from the way is charity,"

and he said:

"Giving your brother a smile is charity, and helping a person load his animal is charity."

Forbidding Evil

What the Bible Says

Whoever corrects a mocker invites insult; whoever rebukes a wicke'd man incurs abuse. **Do not rebuke a mocker** or he will hate you. (Proverbs 9:7,8)

What the Qur'ân Says

Those among the Children of Israel who disbelieved were cursed by the tongue of David and Jesus, son of Mary. That was because they disobeyed and were ever transgressing beyond bounds. **They used not to forbid one another from the wickedness they did.** Verily evil was that they used to do! (Qur'ân, 5:78,79)

Let there arise out of you a band of people inviting to all that is good, enjoining what is right, and forbidding what is wrong and they are the ones who are successful. (Qur'ân, 3:104)

And the believers, men and women, are protecting friends one of another; **they enjoin the right and forbid the wrong,** and they establish worship and they pay the poor-due, and they obey Allâh and His Messenger. On them will Allâh pour his mercy; for Allâh is exalted in power, Wise. (Qur'ân, 9:71)

Commentary

The Bible advises not to rebuke the wicked people in order to avoid hatred and insult. This tolerance towards wickedness resulted in the change and distortion of the religion and the deviation from the teachings of the Prophets in addition to the spread of adultery and evil deeds. Since the Jews didn't use to restrain one another from doing wicked deeds, as soon as a Prophet died they sank into wickedness, adultery and worshiping idols. They did not even wait for the death of Prophet Moses (pbuh); the moment Moses (pbuh) went to the mount, they made the calf and worshiped it.

As for Islam, on the one hand, Allâh says in the Qur'ân: "Let there be no compulsion in religion. (Qur'ân, 2:256). You have the freedom to follow the religion you want and throughout the history of Islam, non-Muslims have enjoyed the highest degree of freedom in the Islamic society; none of the Christians, Jews, Zoroastrians or Hindus has ever been forced to become a Muslim. On the other hand, Islam does not support personal freedom at the expense of Allâh's Laws and the rights of the community. Islam does not give the freedom to insult our creator Allâh the Almighty, nor does it give the freedom to spread wickedness and tempt others to commit evil deeds.

The Qur'ân orders Muslims to command what is good and forbid what is evil. This Islamic teaching is a shield against the storms of wickedness and immorality. Because of this teaching, the religion of Islam has remained pure for fourteen hundred years as if it were preached yesterday, and the Islamic society has remained free from great and shameful sins such as worshiping idols, blasphemy, adultery, fornication, homosexuality, drinking and gambling. Islam does not only want to ensure bodily health, and the cleanness of food and environment, but also wants to purify the society from evil and immoral acts and prevent mental pollution which shakes the belief and corrupts people.

Hypocrisy

What the Bible Says

[Paul said:]

... I make myself a slave to everyone, to win as many as possible. **To the Jews I became like a Jew**, to win the Jews. **To those under the law I became like one under the law** (though I myself am not under the law), so as to win those under the law. **To those not having the law I became like one not having the law**...(1 Corinthians 9:19,21)

Everyone must submit himself to the governing authorities, for there is **no authority** except that which **God has established**.

The authorities that exist have been established by God. Consequently, he who rebels against the authority is rebelling against what God has instituted ... This is also why you pay taxes, for the authorities are God's servants... (Romans 13:1-6)

What the Qur'ân Says

Give to the hypocrites the tidings that there is for them a painful torment. Those who take disbelievers for protectors and friends instead of believers. Do they seek honor, power and glory with them? Verily, then to Allâh belongs all honor, power and glory. (Qur'ân, 4:138-139)

Verily, the hypocrites will be in the lowest depth of the Fire; no helper will you find for them. (Qur'ân, 4:145)

Wine

What the Bible Says

... wine makes life merry, but money is the answer for everything. (Ecclesiastes 10:19)

For the living know that they will die, but the dead know nothing; they have no further reward ... Go, eat your food with gladness, and **drink your wine with a joyful heart**... Whatever your hand finds to do, do it with all your might ... (Ecclesiastes 9:5-10)

Once more he (Jesus) visited Cana in Galilee, **where he had turned water into wine** ... (John 4:46)

What the Qur'ân Says

O you who believe! Intoxicants (all kinds of alcoholic drinks), and gambling, and dedication of stones, and divination by arrows, are an abomination of Satan's handiwork. So avoid it, in order that you may be successful.

Satan wants only to excite enmity and hatred between you with intoxicants (alcoholic drinks) and gambling, and turn you from the remembrance of Allâh and from the prayer. So, will you not then abstain? (Qur'ân, 5:90,91)

Commentary

The Bible does not forbid wine. On the contrary, converting water into wine, **according to the Bible**, was the first miracle of Prophet Jesus (pbuh) (John 2:1-11). Furthermore, bread and wine are offered by the priest during Christian religious service as a sign of Christ's body and blood. Although the Bible **falsely** alleges that **wine** made Prophet Lot (pbuh) commit incest with his two daughters and made Prophet Noah (pbuh) lie naked, there is not a single verse in the Bible that forbids wine–quite the reverse, many verses in the Bible encourage people to drink wine.

Creating a society free from alcohol and other intoxicants is one of the miracles of Islam. Islam prohibits any quantity of alcohol no matter how small it is, because small quantities may well lead to large quantities.

Alcohol is the first step to most crimes and sins. It is a slow poison and can cause fatal diseases. Alcohol takes away self-control and mental ability which distinguishes humans from animals. Many countries realized that alcoholic drinks raise the rate of diseases, poverty, and crime. Therefore, in the beginning of the twentieth century, many countries tried to emulate the Islamic prohibition of alcoholic drinks to protect their societies from this evil. They thought that it was just a matter of making laws. They made prohibition laws and tried to enforce them by imposing strict searches, arrests, fines, imprisonments and executions in addition to using all possible means of media to discourage drinking and warn people against its dangerous effects. However, all their efforts ended in great failure. The prohibition increased people's love for drinking and caused public outrage. Criminals made a lot of money by smuggling, making and selling illegal alcohol. Finally, these countries put an end to the prohibition laws.

In contrast, as soon as the above two Verses of the Qur'ân, which prohibit alcoholic drinks, were revealed, Muslims shouted, "We have abstained! We have abstained!" And they poured out all alcoholic drinks in the streets of Madinah. They did not do that because they were afraid of the law, but because they were lovingly and consciously submitting themselves to the will of their Creator, Allâh the Almighty.

Bribery

What the Bible Says

A **bribe is a charm** to the one who gives it; wherever he turns, **he succeeds**. (Proverbs 17:8)

What the Qur'ân Says

And eat up not one another's property unjustly, nor give bribery to the rulers. (Qur'ân, 2:188)

We will not take a bribe, even though it were on behalf of a near kinsman nor will we hide the testimony of Allâh, for then indeed we should be of the sinful. (Qur'ân, 5:106)

Appendix 1

Examples of the Contradictions in the Bible

And David took from him a thousand chariots, and **seven hundred**[1] horsemen, and twenty thousand footmen ... (2 Samuel 8:4) (KJV)	And David took from him a thousand chariots, and **seven thousand** horsemen, and twenty thousand footmen ... (1 Chronicles 18:4) (KJV)
So Gad came to David, and told him, and said unto him, Shall **seven**[1] **years of famine** come unto thee in thy land? or wilt thou flee three months before thine enemies, while they pursue thee? ... (2 Samuel 24:13) (KJV)	So Gad came to David, and said unto him, Thus saith the Lord, Choose thee. Either **three years' famine**; or three months to be destroyed before thy foes, while that the sword of thine enemies overtaketh thee .. (1 Chronicles 21:11,12) (KJV)
... It held **two thousand** baths. (1 Kings 7:26)	... It held **three thousand** baths. (2 Chronicles 4:5)
And Solomon had **forty**[1] thousand stalls of horses for his chariots, and twelve thousand horsemen. (1 Kings 4:26) (KJV)	And Solomon had **four** thousand stalls for horses and chariots, and twelve thousand horsemen ... (2 Chronicles 9:25) (KJV)
Two and twenty years old was Ahaziah when he began to reign ... (2 Kings 8:26) (KJV)	**Forty and two years**[1] old was Ahaziah when he began to reign ... (2 Chronicles 22:2) (KJV)

(1) The New International Version has changed the number to remove the contradiction.

Jehoiachin was **eighteen** years old when he began to reign, and he reigned in Jerusalem **three months** ... (2 Kings 24:8) (KJV)	Jehoiachin was **eight** years old when he began to reign, and he reigned **three months and ten days** in Jerusalem ... (2 Chronicles 36:9) (KJV)
If I testify about myself, my testimony **is not valid**. (John 5:31)	... Even if I testify on my own behalf, my testimony **is valid** ... (John 8:14)
Leaving that place, Jesus withdrew to the region of Tyre and Sidon. A **Canaanite woman** from that vicinity came to him, crying out, "Lord, Son of David, have mercy on me! My daughter is suffering terribly from demon-possession." (Matthew 15:21,22)	Jesus left that place and went to the vicinity of Tyre ... a woman whose little daughter was possessed by an evil spirit came and fell at his feet. The **woman was a Greek** born in Syrian Phoenicia. She begged Jesus to drive the demon out of her daughter. (Mark 7:24-26)
... **Judas threw the money** into the temple and left. Then he went away and **hanged himself**. The **chief priests** picked up the coins ... **they decided to use the money to buy the potter's field**.. Then what was spoken by Jeremiah the prophet was fulfilled: " They took the thirty silver coins, the price set on him by the people of Israel, and **they used them to buy the potter's field** ... (Matthew 27:5-10)	With the reward he got for his wickedness, **Judas bought a field**: there **he fell headlong**, his body burst open and all his intestines spilled out ... it is written in the book of Psalms, " May his place be deserted; let there be no-one to dwell in it ... (Acts 1:18-20)

And **Jacob the father of Joseph** the husband of Mary, of whom was born Jesus, who is called Christ. (Matthew 1:16)

... He (Jesus) was the **son**, so it was thought, of **Joseph, the son of Heli** (Luke 3:23)

Note: please refer to (Matthew 1:1-16) & (Luke 3:23-34) for 24 more contradictions in the names of Joseph's grandfathers

---

For as Jonah was three days and three nights in the belly of a huge fish, so the son of Man will be **three days and three nights** in the heart of the earth. (Matthew 12:40)

Note: Jesus (pbuh) will be buried for 3 days and 3 nights. ...

he asked for Jesus' body. Then he took it down wrapped it in linen cloth and placed it in a tomb cut in the rock, one in which no-one had yet been laid. It was **Preparation Day, and the Sabbath was about to begin** . (Luke 23:52-54)

After the Sabbath, at dawn on the first day of the week ... He (Jesus) is not here; he has risen... (Matthew 28:1,6)

Note: Jesus (pbuh) was buried for 1 day and 2 nights.

These were his instructions: "Take nothing for the journey **except a staff**–no bread, no bag, no money in your belts. **Wear sandals** but not an extra tunic (Mark 6:8,9)

He told them: "Take nothing for the journey–**no staf**, no bag, no bread, no money, no extra tunic. (Luke 9:3)

These twelve Jesus sent out with the following instructions: ... **take no** bag for the journey, or extra tunic, **or sandals or a staff** ... (Matthew 10:5-10)

... a centurion **came to** him, asking for help. "Lord," he said, "my servant lies at home praralysed and in terrible suffering." Jesus said to him, "I will go and heal him." The centurion replied, "Lord, I do not deserve to have you come under my roof. But just say the word, and my servant will be healed. (Matthew 8:5-8)

Note: The centurion himself asked Jesus for help!

... the centurion **sent friends to say to him**: "Lord, don't trouble yourself, for I do not deserve to have you come under my roof. **That is why I did not even consider myself worthy to come to you**

. But say the word, and my servant will be healed (Luke 7:6,7)

Note: The centurion did not meet Jesus but asked him for help through intermediaries

The above are just few examples of the contradictions in the Bible. Dr. Muhammad Ali Alkhuli, in his book "A Comparison Between the Four Gospels", presented **hundreds** of contradictions in the New Testament and commented:

"Remember that I am giving here mere examples of contradictions in the NT (New Testament) ... One may argue that these are minor points of disagreement. In answer to this argument, I would emphasize that with God's word, we do not expect neither minor nor major contradictions because God is the Perfect, the All-Knowing. Contradictions in the NT prove that the NT cannot be God's word." (Dar Alfalah, 1998, p 41)

Appendix 2

What the Bible Says about the Coming of Prophet Mohammed (pbuh)

There are many prophecies about Prophet Jesus (pbuh) in the Old Testament and many Prophets gave the glad tidings of his coming. Both Christians and Muslims believe that the awaited Christ was Prophet Jesus (pbuh). Muslims, in compliance with the Qur'ân, believe that Jesus (pbuh) was a great Messenger of Allâh, that he brought the dead to life by Allâh's leave and that he was born miraculously.

There are also prophecies about the coming of Prophet Muhammad (pbuh) and the Qur'ân praises those who acknowledge these prophecies and follow Prophet Muhammad (pbuh):

Those who follow the Messenger, the Prophet who can neither read nor write (Muhammad) **whom they find written with them in the Torah and the Injeel (Gospel),** he commands them for that which is right and forbids them from that which is wrong; he makes lawful for them all good things and prohibits for them the evil things; he releases them from their heavy burdens and from the fetters (bindings) that were upon them. (Qur'ân, 7:157)

There are tens of prophecies about Prophet Muhammad (pbuh) in the Old Testament and the New Testament. For the sake of brevity, only two prophecies are discussed:

Prophecy

The Lord said to me (Moses): "What they say is good. I will raise up for them a **prophet** **like you** from **among their brothers**; I will put my words in his mouth, and he will tell them everything I command him. If anyone does not listen to my **words** that the prophet speaks **in my name**, I myself will call him to account." (Deuteronomy 18:17-19)

Commentary

- **from among their brothers**

This Prophet could not be any Israelite Prophet because the verse does not say "from them" but it says "from among their brothers". The brothers of the Israelites are the Arabs who are the descendants of Ishmael the son of Abraham and the brother of Isaac.

- **like you**

There are many similarities between Prophet Moses (pbuh) and Prophet Muhammad (pbuh):

Comparison	Moses (pbuh)	Muhammad (pbuh)
Birth	Normal	Normal
Marriage/ Children	Married and had children	Married and had children
Death	Died and was buried	Died and was buried
Law	Brought new Law	Brought new Law
Acceptance by his people	Accepted	Accepted

Furthermore, the following verse indicates that the Jews were waiting for the coming of the promised Christ [Jesus (pbuh)] and the promised Prophet [(Muhammad (pbuh)]:

Now some Pharisees who had been sent questioned him (John the Baptist), "Why then do you baptize if you are not the **Christ**, nor Elijah, nor the **Prophet**?" (John 1:24,25)

Prophecy

The Servant of the Lord

"Here is **my servant**, whom I uphold, my chosen one in whom I delight; I will put my Spirit on him and **he will bring justice to the nations.** He will not shout or cry out, or raise his voice in the streets. A bruised reed he will not break, and a smouldering wick he will not snuff out. In faithfulness he will bring forth justice; **he will not falter or be discouraged till he establishes justice on earth. In his law** the islands will put their hope."...

Let the desert and its towns raise their voices; let the settlements where Kedar lives rejoice. Let the people of Sela sing for joy; let them shout from the mountaintops. Let them give glory to the Lord...

But those who trust in idols, who say to images, 'You are our gods,' will be turned back in utter shame. (Isaiah 42:1-17)

Commentary

This prophecy is a very clear prophecy. It does not fit but Prophet Muhammad (pbuh). In fact, it is a clear description of Prophet Muhammad (pbuh), his ministry, his followers and his enemies.

- **my servant**

Prophet Muhammad and all the other Prophets (pbut) are

servants of Allâh. They did not have any divine qualities, as they were all humans created by Allâh like the rest of mankind.

- **he will bring justice to the nations**

Prophet Muhammad (pbuh) was sent as a mercy and guidance for all humans:

And We have not sent you (O Muhammad) except as a giver of glad tidings and a warner to all mankind (Qur'ân, 34:28)

Prophet Muhammad (pbuh) brought the religion of Islam which made people of all nations brothers entitled to equal rights without any racism or discrimination and established a society in which justice prevails; Muslims and non-Muslims are equally treated. Furthermore, Islam has shown the height of tolerance towards other religions, which is admitted even by its enemies.

- **he will not falter or be discouraged till he establishes justice on earth.**

Despite the strong hostility of his enemies, Prophet Muhammad (pbuh) had not been weakened or discouraged until he overcame his enemies, spread Islam and established justice.

- **In his _law_ the islands will put their hope**

Prophet Muhammad (pbuh) is the Prophet who brought a new law which is the Islamic Law. All Israelite Prophets after Prophet Moses (pbuh) did not bring a new law as they maintained the Law of Prophet Moses (pbuh).

- **Let the desert and its towns raise their voices; let the settlements where Kedar lives rejoice. Let the people of Sela sing for joy; let them shout from the mountaintops. Let them give glory to the Lord...**

The word 'Kedar' confirms that this servant is Prophet Muhammad (pbuh) because he is the only Prophet who descended from Kedar the son of Ishmael the son of Abraham:

These are the names of the sons of Ishmael, listed in the order of their birth: Nebaioth the firstborn of Ishmael, **Kedar** .. (Genesis 25:13)

Furthermore, except for Prophet Abraham and Ishmael (pbut), the descendants of Kedar had not followed any other Prophet until the coming of Prophet Muhammad (pbuh). After they followed Prophet Muhammad (pbuh) and embraced Islam, they started raising their voices from the minarets of mosques five times a day giving glory to the Lord and bearing witness that there is no god but He. They also started shouting from the mountaintops during the annual pilgrimage praising and thanking Allâh.

- **But those who trust in idols, who say to images, 'You are our gods,' will be turned back in utter shame.**

Prophet Muhammad (pbuh) and his followers defeated the idol worshipers of Arabia who used to say to images: "You are our gods." He destroyed their idols and made religion pure for Allâh.

What They Say about the Qur'ân

I studied a Muslim translation of the Holy Qur'ân, and was astounded to read such noble precepts and inspiring passages, such wise and practical advice for everyday life. It made me wonder why I had been taught that Muhammad was a false prophet, and how I had not heard the truth about this wonderful religion earlier.[1]

Hasan V Mathews

The Holy Qur'ân, some passages of which I read, simply struck me with wonder, for I had the idea that there was nothing to rival the Bible. I found, however, that I was hopelessly mistaken in this. Indeed, the Holy Qur'ân, is so full of truths, and its teachings so practical and free from dogmatic tenets and mysteries, that I was daily being drifted into the religion of 'Peace & Love' which Islam certainly is.[2]

Mumin Abdur-Razzaque, Selliah, Ceylon

My Opinion of Islam was not favorable one before I read the Holy Qur'ân. I took the Holy Book with curiosity, and opened it with scorn, expecting to find in it horrible errors, blasphemies, superstitions and contradictions. I was biased, but I was also very young and my heart had no time to harden completely yet. I went through the Surah (Chapter) reluctantly at the beginning, eagerly then and finally with a desperate thirst for Truth. Then in the

---

(1) Muhammad Haneef Shahid, Why Islam Is Our Only Choice, (Darussalam Publications, 1996), p. 90.
(2) Ibid, p. 91.

greatest moment of my life, Allâh gave me His guidance and led me from superstitions to truth, from darkness to light, from Christianity to Islam.[1]

Saifuddin Dirk Walter, Mosing USA

The Bible I always heartily disliked it gave me neither comfort, consolation, nor the smallest help whatever. When I grew up, I found it a mass of contradictions, extra ordinary fables and impossibilities that one felt disgusted and saddened instead of being helped and comforted. The Bible is the result of a collaboration of dozens of different authors. The Holy Book of Islam the Qur'ân, on the contrary, has come to us through only one man, namely the Holy Prophet Muhammad. It has never been altered, twisted, paraphrased and transcribed as the Bible, but has remained true to its original copy. The Qur'ân appealed to me. The doctrine of Islam appealed to me.[2]

Ameena Annie Spieget, England

The superiority of the Qur'ân over the Bible to me lay in its all-embracing universality in contrast to the narrow, rigid, nationalism of the Jewish Scriptures which is one of the reasons, why Jews to this day have never been able to outgrow their tribal mentality.[3]

Maryam Jameelah Begum (Formerly Margaret Marcus)

The Qur'ân, while inviting us to cultivate science, itself contains many observations on natural phenomena and includes explanatory details which are seen to be in total agreement with modern scientific data. There is no equal to this in the Judeo-Christian Revelation.[4]

Maurice Bucaille

---

(1) Ibid, p. 92.
(2) Muhammad Haneef Shahid, Why Islam Is Our Only Choice, (Darussalam Publications, 1996), p. 93.
(3) Ibid, p. 93.
(4) Maurice Bucaille, The Bible, The Qur'an And Science (Kazi Publications), p. 116.

It seems to me that Muhammad was a very ordinary man. He could not read, didn't know [how] to write. In fact, he was an illiterate. And we're talking about twelve (actually about fourteen) hundred years ago. You have someone illiterate making profound pronouncements and statements and that are amazingly accurate about scientific nature. And I personally cant's see how this could be a mere chance. There are too many accuracies and, like Dr. Moore, I have no difficulty in my mind that this is a divine inspiration or revelation which led him to these statements.[1]

Dr. T. B. N. Persaud,
Professor of Anatomy
University of Manitoba, Canada

I think, that not only there is no conflict between genetics and religion but, in fact, religion can guide science by adding revelation to some of the traditional scientific approaches, that there exist statements in the Qur'ân shown centuries later to be valid, which support knowledge in the Qur'ân having been derived from God.[2]

Dr. Joe Leigh Simpson
Chairman of the Department of Obstetrics and Gynecology
Baylor College of Medicine
Houston, Texas, USA

Whereas monumental errors are to be found in the Bible, I could not find a single error in the Qur'an. I had to stop and ask myself: if a man was the author of the Qur'an, How could he gave written facts in the Seventh century A.D. that today are shown to be in keeping with modern scientific knowledge?[3]

Maurice Bucaille

---

(1) I. A. Ibrahim, A Brief Illustrated Guide to Understanding Islam (Darussalam, Publishers and Distributors, Houston, Texas, USA), p. 27.
(2) Ibid, p. 29.
(3) Maurice Bucaille, The Bible, The Qur'an And Science (Kazi Publications), p. 120.

Well, then, if the Koran were his (Muhammad's) own composition, other men could rival it. Let them produce ten Verses like it. If they could not (and it is obvious that they could not), then let them accept the Koran as an outstanding existential miracle.[1]

H. A. R. Gibb

---

(1) Quoted by Dr Norlain Dindang Mababaya and Mamarinta-Umar P. Mababaya, Holy Qu'raan: The Book of Guidance,(International Islamic Publishing House, 1995), p 6.

References

Holy Bible, New International Version. International Bible Society. 2000.

Bucaille, Maurice. The Bible The Qur'an And Science. Lahore. Kazi Publications.

Ibrahim,I. A. A Brief Illustrated Guide to Understanding Islam. Houston, Texas, USA. Darussalam. Publishers and Distributors.

Shahid, Muhammad Haneef. Why Islam Is Our Only Choice. Riyadh. Darussalam Publications. 1996.

Deedat, Ahmed. Is the Bible God's Word. Riyadh. International Islamic Publishing House. 1998.

Badawi, Jamal. Muhammad in The Bible. Riyadh. International Islamic Publishing House. 1995.

Abdel Azeem, Sheriff. Women In Islam Versus Women in The Judaeo-Christian Tradition: The Myth & The Reality. Eastern Province, Saudi Arabia. World Assembly of Muslim Youth.

Abdalati, Hammudah. Islam in Focus. Indianapolis, Indiana. American Trust Publications. 1975.

Mawdudi, Abul A'la. Towards Understanding Islam. London. The Islamic Foundation. 1998.

Kutub, Muhammed. Islam The Misunderstood Religion. Salimiah-Kuwait. International Islamic Federation of Student Organizations. 1991.

Alkhuli, Muhammad Ali. the Need for Islam. Swaileh, Jordan. Alfalah House. 1998.

Aziz-Us-Samad, Ulfat. Islam and Christianity. International Islamic Federation of Student Organizations. 1997.